Issues in the Social Sciences Series: 3

Series Editor: Anne Boran

Decoding Discrimination

In the Same Series

1. Crime: Fear or Fascination? edited by Anne Boran

2. Gender in Flux; edited by Anne Boran and Bernadette Murphy

Decoding Discrimination

*Papers from a Conference held at
University College Chester,
November 2002*

Edited by Mark Bendall and Brian Howman

Chester Academic Press

First published 2006
by Chester Academic Press
University of Chester
Parkgate Road
Chester CH1 4BJ

Printed and bound in the UK by the
Learning Resources Print Unit,
University of Chester
Cover designed by the
Learning Resources Graphics Team,
University of Chester

The foreword and editorial material
© University of Chester, 2006
The individual chapters
© the respective authors, 2006

All Rights Reserved
No part of this publication may be reproduced, stored in a retrieval system or transmitted in any form or by any means without the prior permission of the copyright owner, other than as permitted by current UK copyright legislation or under the terms and conditions of a recognised copyright licensing scheme

A catalogue record for this book is available from the British Library

CONTENTS

Contributors — vii

Foreword — xiii

Acknowledgements — xv

Introduction — 1
Mark Bendall and Brian Howman

1. Lifting the Veil of Religious and Cultural Identities — 12
   Marie Parker-Jenkins

2. Growing Old Invisibly: Older Viewers Talk Television — 46
   Tim Healey and Karen Ross

3. Is the World Moving?: Changing Women, Unchanged Men in Post-Industrial Britain — 75
   Sara Delamont

4. The Social Construction of Stigma in Health Care Settings — 94
   Tom Mason and Elizabeth Mason-Whitehead

5. Class and Inequality in Contemporary Britain — 127
   Mike Savage

6. Disability, Discrimination and
   Disabled People
   Colin Barnes
   148

7. Rebellious Subcultures: Fashioning
   the Revolution in a Revolutionary
   Fashion or Vehicles of Resistance
   en Route to Conformity?
   Joanna Elloy
   180

FOREWORD

A fine line has been drawn in this book between the determinism of old-fashioned structuralism and the nuanced fluidity of post-modernism. Each author manages to avoid the pitfalls of these two extremes. Nevertheless, social structures that create and perpetuate inequality are the main topic within each chapter. I read the book with great pleasure, aware that social inequality and discrimination need to be unpicked before they can be publicly challenged. This book unpicks several topics, including disability, fashion, gender, and class, with a vengeance.

The book is about inequality and discrimination. These topics are notoriously hard to document. One old-fashioned option is to presuppose a measurable concept of inequality – e.g. class – and then move into statistical analysis. Similarly, if discrimination is measured simply by the net outcomes, then it becomes an easy subject for us to study. For instance, in the study of the gender pay gap we can measure the gap as 42% for part-time working women in the UK and 20% for women overall. Part-time working women earn 42% less than the average male full-time wage (in Pounds per hour; 2005 data; see www.dti.gov.uk for documentation). Full-time working women earn 20% less. But these figures belie the complexity of the causes behind "discrimination" and they tend to oversimplify the reality of discrimination and its contexts. In this book, the contexts get a strong qualitative and historical treatment. The statistical side is less prominent because glib assumptions are avoided.

This book is one in a series sponsored by the University of Chester. By making a concerted effort at contributing to the flow of new academic ideas, the University of Chester (newly established in 2005) and the linked Chester Academic Press are part of a solid, useful and worthwhile tradition. New presses produce material which established large-scale publishers might not want to publish, as they tend to move away from substantive perspectives on the value of published work towards more commercial ones, creating an atmosphere within which commissioning editors must justify their "results" each year and help their firm make a profit.

This can result in textbooks being preferred to monographs, as they sell larger numbers of copies, but with the risk of a dumbing-down of content. Also, monographs by a single author may be preferred to edited volumes. This may lead to the publishing of high quality works that mark out new areas of research, but with less possibility of face-to-face argumentation, team-working or sustained critique.

The University of Chester has created a space for critique and negotiation, within which high quality research can be published in edited volumes, and an academic environment within which students and staff can interact with regional and national networks of interested researchers. This is to everyone's benefit.

The editors of this volume are to be congratulated for compiling a sensible, unrepetitive, thorough, and extremely high quality set of papers, based upon their annual Conference. A full summary of the work is provided in the Introduction. My Foreword can therefore remain short and congratulatory, and I urge the reader to peruse the contents and buy the book.

Wendy Olsen
Cathie Marsh Centre for Census and Survey Research,
University of Manchester
January 2006

ACKNOWLEDGEMENTS

At the risk of becoming a lachrymose Oscar speech-writer, thanks professionally to Anne Boran for getting and keeping the project going effectively and Peter Williams for so carefully stewarding it through. Thanks go, too, to Professor Mike Richards, Dr Graham McCann and Carolyn Dovey.

More personally, "respect'" to Jem, Veronica and Peter, as well as Ellie and Evie; to Phil, Emma, Caroline, Annette, Nik, Gareth, Peter M., Jon T. from school days, and all the other good-hearted people I have been lucky enough to know, who only discriminate against the small-minded.

MB

I would like to express heartfelt thanks to all my colleagues in the Department of Social and Communications Studies at Chester for their support in this and other projects. I am also grateful for the support provided by my friends, parents and sister during the period spent editing this volume. In terms of my physical and mental well-being, it has been a trying time, but I survived.

BH

INTRODUCTION

Discrimination, difference and inequality are master-concepts, useful to those working in the fields of criminology, communications and social science. Our socio-historical world is structured around these divisions and disparities. In an era of domestic and international terrorism, understanding these divisions and where possible seeking to reduce them are ever more urgent critical interventions, which academics and students can make in opposition to those who would ignite divisions for political gain. This text is a modest contribution to that critical intervention.[1]

---

[1] Polemical contributions that were also made to the conference, but not to this volume, included one by R. K. Corkhill, Chief Minister of the Isle of Man, who gave us a rhetorical, political speech on the alleged problems of positive discrimination. He highlighted in particular the perils of social engineering in established universities, some of which had, he felt, discriminated against the more affluent applicant in favour of students from deprived socio-economic backgrounds; because of current admissions policies they had, he claimed, more readily been given a place. This was a form of social exclusion of the reverse kind, but a no less pernicious one, Corkhill asserted. As academic rather than political texts were needed for this book, the conference team were unable to include this contribution, but thank the Chief Minister for his speech.

In addition, Celius Victor looked at constructions of citizenship, the invention of Britishness, and the issue of race. He took a broad historical sweep, tracing trajectories from the slave trade to current stigmatisation of the non-White in the UK. Though the conference team appreciated the speech, we were sadly unable to include it in the final volume, as these themes were essentially repeated and extended with academic references by our keynote speaker, Professor Marie Parker-Jenkins.

Decoding Discrimination

The University of Chester's annual conference was dedicated to interrogating these relations of inequality by aiming to decode the riddle of discrimination. Could it be best explained by adopting a structuralist analysis implied by a deconstruction of the term "Inequality", or by a more post-modern approach related to themes such as distinction and difference? This book is a selected compilation of those contributions which most closely cohered with the intellectual direction of the text. One of the themes of this book, how individuals, cohorts and systems can treat people as if they are inferior because they are in some way different, remains intensely relevant to the twenty-first century. A reader only has to open a newspaper to see evidence of discrimination, scratching away at the crevices of society like an infestation. At the start of 2005, examples abounded of those in powerful positions making comments that echoed the prejudices of earlier generations. In terms of gender, Lawrence Summers, President of Harvard University, sparked a media firestorm by arguing that men outperform women in mathematics and science because of biological superiority and by asserting that discrimination is no longer a career barrier for female academics. Yet, during his presidency, the number of jobs offered by Harvard to women has dropped from 36% to 13%.[2] If an enlightened member of the élite can make antiquated statements, it shows how much cultural work still needs to be done in society at large.

In terms of race, pictures of British soldiers standing on stricken Iraqi captives recalled colonial narratives of dominance over, and disdain for, non-White peoples. This continues the historical process of cultural imperialism, which pervades the discourses considered in this text. The

---

[2] *The Washington Times*, January 19, 2005, p. A02.

Introduction

focus of this book is largely a Western one and it examines in historical terms relatively recent experiences of discrimination. It traces patterns of prejudice via prisms of race, gender, mental illness, disability and age, and it examines the class divisions that cut across or underpin these issues, and explores subcultures within, and across, classes. Some writers emphasise one theme, such as class, without reference to race; others emphasise gender, rather than class. An ideal-type study might confront all of these variables, though in practice a more limited focus is necessary for manageable individual research. These studies offer excellent surveys of research by experts in their field.

The areas focused on in this book are not exhaustive of discrimination and difference. The systematic verbal and physical abuse of sexual minorities is not covered here, nor are the particular challenges facing transsexuals, for example. (Readers may wish to turn to the text on *Gender in Flux* in this same series for an analysis of this issue). Whilst ageism is examined in relation to the mass media, discrimination against children lies outside the remit of this project. Though the problems suffered by racial minorities are considered, prejudice coming from those groups towards the Caucasian majority is not. In fact, research on discrimination tends to assume that prejudice is directed out from majority groups to vulnerable ones. It needs to engage too with the assumptions of minority groups; discrimination can be a two-way, reactive process.

Hence this text itself might be accused of discriminating against those groups which did not find their way into it. However, it is a selective group of studies and areas of omission may be tackled later in the series. The themes included and the forces at work within them do, however, have a strong commonality with those themes that are omitted.

Decoding Discrimination

Enoch Powell's rivers of blood prophecy has failed to come true, yet discrimination around the matrix of religion and race has, far from eroding, in fact become a literally more explosive issue in a post-9/11, post-suicide bomber Britain. The fact that the former leading BBC commentator and Labour MP Robert Kilroy-Silk, now leader of the vehemently anti-immigration Veritas political party, can comment that Arabs have contributed nothing to culture, other than arm amputation; the fact that the British National Party has had more electoral success with its racist agenda in recent years; and that allegedly even the Chief Inspector of Schools, David Bell, can target Muslim (but not Christian) schools as potentially segregationist[3], indicate that Britain is engaged in a heated dialogue about race and religiosity. The inadvisability of Bell's comment is highlighted, arguably, by the violent sectarianism amongst and between Christians in Northern Ireland, the West of Scotland and other parts of the United Kingdom. This debate has become a pan-European one, with the French Government trying to ban Muslim headscarves and with the Netherlands, hitherto known as a haven of inclusiveness, dealing with the burning of Muslim schools and the assassination of Theo van Gogh, a cultural leader critical of domestic violence in the Muslim community.

Professor Parker-Jenkins decodes discrimination by examining freedom of religion and belief, dimensions of culture and ethnicity, and what she terms "cultural discrimination". She makes the point that self-description is primarily an expression of a sense of belonging, whether through choice of dress such as a *hijab*, or choice of school. Identity is framed around both exclusion and aspiration. Culture is not defined by fixed boundaries and some Asian

---

[3] *education.guardian.co.uk/faithschools/story/0, 13882, 1392833, 00.html.*

Introduction

communities are doubly stigmatised for their ethnicity and their colour.

Parker-Jenkins points to the complexity of the race-ethnicity matrix, the need to move beyond crude categorisation. She emphasises that religion is more important to the self-identity of the Muslim and perhaps the Sikh and Hindu psyche than race. Assimilation is sometimes demanded, and this is part of the arsenal of discrimination. Ethnic communities have become energised, politicised and radicalised in the wake of September 11, as evidenced, for example, by Muslim women protesting openly against the Bush-Blair war in Eurasia. Parker-Jenkins also discusses the legal dimensions to the issue; laws can protect and they can exclude. It is how they are implemented (for example, by police officers) that can contribute to the sense that a White state casts Asian males under suspicion. Citizenship can also be seen as a coercive force that serves to restrict membership to the imagined community of the nation, with both major British political parties apparently competing to see who can appear toughest in shoring up a notion of pure Britishness. Parker-Jenkins's account could not be more timely, then, in trying to make sense of the knot of race, ethnicity and discrimination, especially in the wake of the bombs in London of the 7th of July, 2005.

The challenges of old age face all ethnicities. Whilst the visible markers of race and religiosity bring prejudicial attention, it is the comparative invisibility of the "Third Age" in the media which troubles Healey and Ross. Often, the aged character is tokenistic and thinly drawn, even though the grey vote makes up a sizeable swathe of the population; by 2050, one person in three in Europe will be over 60. This study foregrounds the experiences of older people themselves, detailing their experiences of stereotyped delineations of the aged on TV: archetypes of the eccentric, the mockable and the vulnerable. Explanations for these tropes of age by the senior citizens interviewed are, by contrast, robust and energetic. They recognise the demographic target of advertisers and discern the comparative youth of TV executives. Future studies, building on this valuable contribution to the volume, could perhaps explore old age refracted through the prism of race and sexuality.

Women tend to make up the bulk of those suffering from the social problem of pensioner poverty, and it is women that form the focus of Delamont's study of the nature of change in the post-Fordist United Kingdom. Delamont asks if women have changed whilst men have been in stasis. This accessible study charts the course of, and threats to, feminism from evolutionary psychology through to modish post-modernism. In the final analysis (an analysis that elides nicely with Savage's chapter) the significance of class as the crucial marker of distinction and division is emphasised: gender cuts comparatively less ice. Cultural reproduction leads Delamont to argue that the lives of nineteenth century women were not enormously different from those of the early twenty-first century. Future work could build on this key study by adding permutations of region, race or sexual orientation to the analysis.

What unites many of these studies is their analysis of the attitude of the herd as it turns to examine the marginal figure and that of the marginal figure as it tries to join or shun the herd. On closer inspection, the human herd itself splits into different hides.

When the attention of the majority is hostile, whether in terms of ageism, sexism or class prejudice, a key explanatory concept is stigma and a critical effect of this is social exclusion. Mason and Mason-Whitehead use Goffman's study to explain how a stranger with some

Introduction

noticeable difference is marked as tainted, with individuals becoming reduced to the distinctive feature that leads to stigmatisation. Individuals become deviant, not necessarily because of any intrinsic quality, but because of the label tied around them like a steel lasso. Uncovering the signs of difference, whether physical or cultural, is seen as revealing a truth about the body or the culture, a truth used to confirm difference and justify discrimination.

As the contents of the chapters in this volume illustrate, the issues surrounding discrimination are varied, and they manifest themselves in a number of complex, interrelated and overlapping ways. However, in this apparently post-modern age, it is easy (if not excusable), to dismiss traditional notions of discrimination by social class. Mike Savage tackles this conundrum in an effective way, by discussing the "paradox of class", whereby people lack awareness of their position in society and seem largely to accept the view that we are living in a classless society: a political line promoted by the leaders of the three major political parties in Great Britain, and supported by the media. Whilst members of the working class, by and large, no longer identify themselves as such, the inequalities they suffer are no less profound. Indeed, it is argued that this blurring of societal boundaries, including those of social class, only serves to exacerbate the problems of discrimination and inequality. Savage argues with a great deal of conviction and justification that this paradox of class leads to an even greater dislocation from society, manifested in part through a decreasing involvement of working class people in political, community and voluntary organisations.

In the light of the above, two concepts become immediately apparent. Firstly, that it is time to reintroduce notions of people's relationship with the political and economic system and to re-adopt the model of societal superstructure and infrastructure, in order to recognise polarisation by social class, which clever politicking around notions of classlessness seeks to hide. We must understand this dropping out of public life, this apparent deficit of social capital, as a symptom of structural divisions within society, not as a series of "individual problems". Secondly, if members of the working class do not see themselves as such, then we might argue that further discrimination by gender, ethnicity, sexual preference, physical ability, etcetera is inevitable, or at least likely. A person's relationship to the economic and political structure helps shape, to a great extent, their ability to make their way through life. If lack of individual success (however that is defined) cannot be explained through traditional notions of class difference and discrimination, then we will potentially look for other causes: other enemies, so to speak. We can, perhaps, see evidence of this in the increasing working class support for far-Right political movements and in the growth of religious intolerance, most especially today in the form of Islamophobia. Fears of Islamophobia, as evidenced by attacks on mosques, have predictably intensified after the first suicide attacks on British shores by Muslims born in the UK.

It follows then that, instead of broad fundamental structural problems, those at the sharp end of class inequality will, in the absence of awareness of their social class, move towards *blaming* other groupings, such as those outlined above. We can see this process at work in the chapters by Colin Barnes and Joanna Elloy, who discuss incisively discrimination by disability and lifestyle respectively. As Colin Barnes asserts, disabled people's involvement in key areas of political, economic and cultural life are seriously constrained. He argues that, without a fundamental change in societal values, this

Introduction

situation can only deteriorate; diversity needs to be celebrated, not rejected. In the light of Mike Savage's conclusions about declining class awareness, together with the increasing individualisation of people's problems rather than their location within failing societal structures, the position of all *minority* groups will be very vulnerable indeed.

We see related processes at work when discussing lifestyle and "rebellious subcultures". Joanna Elloy argues that these subcultures are in fact subverted, in that their symbols become part of mainstream culture. An explanation for this, perhaps, lies in the perception of yesterday's hippies, mods, rockers and punks being today's teachers, lawyers, accountants and corporate traders. Further, post-modernists could point to the subversion of these rebellious subcultures as evidence of a lack of boundaries, of the breaking down of barriers; in short, a largely positive process and a move towards a "heterogeneous post-modern society". However, the fact that chain stores stock (and profit from) clothing adorned with Che Guevara's face cannot credibly be seen as an acceptance of his principles, but obviously as a definite subversion of them.

Elloy effectively points out the complex relationship between capitalism and rebellious subcultures which, if considered alongside Mike Savage's notion of the paradox of class, leads us to draw some pessimistic conclusions about the success of attempts to combat discrimination. This is because, following the post-modernists' analyses, individual problems of inequality are just that: individual. We are drawn away from analysing and understanding the structures which create these inequalities. If we also consider Colin Barnes's assertion that disability is largely a constructed phenomenon, then a view of society which determines that its political, economic and cultural structures play no part in discriminatory processes not only avoids the issues – it actually increases social dislocation and exclusion.

Not all discrimination is evidenced with a bruise or bloodshed. It might leave no outward marks on the sufferer; inwardly, it can be cancerous and hard to treat. Sometimes it is tonal: a sigh; a smirk – the subtle semiotics of paracommunication. Sometimes it is traced in after-work gossip or patterns of exclusion within work. Individuals find ways to signify disapproval subliminally, even when they are qualified to discern patterns of discrimination and even when they have experienced it themselves. Games are played and jokes are cracked with very serious consequences for the perpetrators of discrimination and for its victims. Silences can be as injurious as shouting and deliberate absences as painful as looming presences. Oppressive structures take longer to erode. If, however, as empowered agents, we can use our critical consciousness to challenge discrimination rather than to reproduce it maliciously, then the pillars of institutionalised discrimination can be abraded incrementally, until the whole edifice collapses - rather like a sturdy fence splintering apart after an army of termites has marched through it.

To sum up, what is clear from the various contributors to this conference is that inequalities in this "post-modern age" continue to be caused by social, political and economic constructs. Whilst we dare not dismiss post-modernist analyses entirely, we must be careful not to let the dust storms of deconstruction cloud empirical realities. Social forces and structures are still at work, creating inequality, exclusion, public squalor and private despair.[4]

---

[4] That so many can die of starvation in Western Africa, immediately after and despite a global, mediazed "Make Poverty History" campaign

Introduction

We ignore them at our own peril. The sphere of society, and the network of communications within it, beats to the discordant rhythm of disempowerment. To write of these relations in terms of playfulness, easy identity-transformations and endless relativism, as some post-modernists do, is irresponsible. In some ways, this is an era when, as Baudrillard would have it in *Simulations*, we cannot tell the difference between image and reality; when there is resistance to all-explaining metanarratives; and when cynicism rather than social responsibility shapes much popular and often academic discourse. This text aims to be a small critical intervention to all that. Discrimination is not just a story; it is alive and kicking. One can tell by the kicking. It is, finally, our responsibility as students of society, criminology, communication studies and counselling to make sense of the symbolic (and actual) violence represented by discrimination. It is, we feel, an individual and a social responsibility, beyond analysing it, to *do* something, however modest, about it.

---

and despite a G8 summit dedicated in part to tackling African poverty, emphasises how questions of inequality remain pressing. (BBC World Service report, July 25, 2005).

1

LIFTING THE VEIL OF RELIGIOUS AND CULTURAL IDENTITIES

Marie Parker-Jenkins

Identity is socially and culturally "located" in time and space and inflected by rejection, displacement and desire. (Ball, Maguire, & Macrae, 2000, p. 24).

This chapter is concerned with religious identity and the experience of discrimination. There has been considerable progress in establishing the legal status of the right to freedom of religion and belief during the past few decades in Europe and elsewhere, and the entitlement is officially recognised in domestic and international law. This tradition is perpetuated and sustained in schooling, as well as by the family. In this chapter, I review the concept of freedom of religion and belief, what we mean by a religious identity, and the relationship between religion and ethnicity. As a way of examining the concept of religion, the discussion draws on some of my research projects, which have explored the nature of religious discrimination, especially as experienced by Muslims as victims. Finally, I conclude by exploring the wider issue of religion with regard to notions of citizenship, in the aftermath of September 11th and political insecurity.

Lifting the Veil of Religious and Cultural Identities

Freedom of Religion and Belief

At the outset it is useful to consider what we mean by "freedom of religion and belief". The capacity to believe is a defining feature of human beings; it is a characteristic which has found expression in religions and ideologies throughout history (Smart, 1989; Bowker, 1997). Most countries recognise freedom of religion and have laws which relate to this freedom, but there are varying degrees of the right in terms of principle or practice. The United Nations *Declaration of Human Rights* (1948) states:

> Everyone has the right to freedom of thought, conscience and religion; this right includes freedom to change his religion or belief, and freedom, either alone or in community with others and in public or private, to manifest his religion or belief in teaching, practice, worship and observance. (Article 18)

Protection of this freedom is not restricted to religion, but applies also to atheism and the right *not* to profess any belief. It also covers freedom of thought, conscience and personal convictions and a commitment to belief, whether manifested as an individual or in a community with others. Importantly, freedom of religion is wide-ranging and does not refer to traditional world religions only. As such, new religious organisations or religious minorities are entitled to equal protection (Barker, 1989; Barrett, 1996). In reality, however, the right to freedom of religious belief may only exist as rhetoric and in practice there can be intolerance shown by the state, by individuals, and among religious groups.

Decoding Discrimination

Clarification of terminology is useful here, for "religion" is commonly interpreted by the UN *Declaration* as being broad in scope, compared with the narrowness of historical interpretation, and it incorporates freedom of "thought and conscience". The concept of "beliefs" is a broader category than religion and can incorporate political and ideological views, as well as spiritual or moral views on life. The word "faith" is often used by religions themselves and refers to a way of life rather than a hierarchical structure. Faith groups can be said to share a "truth", a knowledge that they wish to share with others and through which they examine their own problems and those of society in general (Coward, Hinnells, & Williams, 2000). Their understanding of inclusion and the global nature of religion mean that throughout history they have spanned many cultures (Hinnells, 1997). Faith, identity and culture are interrelated, with subtle layers of meaning, and different groups maintain their cultural heritage differently. Conversely, "secular" means "not concerned with or related to religion", and there are at times difficulties if secular educationalists do not understand religious educationalists and in some cases challenge the view that there is a place for religion in school (Humanist Philosophers' Group, 2001). However, despite the differences between religious and secular teachers, there tends to be a shared consensus on the critical place of moral values in the educational process.

Parents have the right to raise their children according to their religious convictions or conscience, passing down religious belief from one generation to another in the home, without interference by the state. This is reflected in European law as follows:

Lifting the Veil of Religious and Cultural Identities

No person shall be denied the right to education. In the exercise of any function, which it assumes in relation to education and teaching, the State shall respect the right of parents to ensure such education and teaching in conformity with their own religious and philosophical convictions. (Council of Europe, Article 2, Protocol 1, 1950)

In school, children have the right to receive an education in matters of religion or belief which is in conformity with the wishes of their parents, and so educational settings are frequently the place where issues of religious identity are confronted. Importantly, the state is not obliged to provide schools which meet the religious beliefs of parents, but instead to respect the liberty of parents to establish schools which reflect their religious beliefs (Parker-Jenkins, 1995).

It should be stated, however, that rights are not absolute and can be subject to time, circumstance and place. So, in this case, the rights of the parents are balanced by the requirement that religious freedom must not be injurious to the child. In addition, the child should have access to education that protects it from intolerance and encourages a respect for the beliefs of others. The United Nations *Convention on the Rights of the Child* (1989), for example, stipulates that there must be respect for the child's right to freedom of thought, conscience and religion as the child gets older. Significantly, therefore, the law recognises the rights of the parents and the rights of the child, and there are occasions when these sets of rights may be in conflict.

There is also a distinction made between the right to have religious convictions, an unconditional right, and the freedom to manifest those beliefs. The concept of freedom of manifestation of belief can cover a broad range of activities, such as the building of places of worship, the displaying of religious symbols and the choice of religious holidays and days of rest. Furthermore,

> The observance and practice of religion may include not only ceremonial acts, but also such customs as the observance of dietary regulations, the wearing of distinctive clothing or head coverings and the use of a particular language customarily spoken by a group .... the practice and teaching of religion ....the freedom to choose their religious leaders, priests and teachers, the right to establish seminaries or religious schools and the freedom to prepare and distribute religious texts or publications. (Boyle & Sheen, 1997, p. 7)

The right to wear distinctive clothing, head covering or veils is a point raised later with regard to my research projects. In interpreting this right, Boyle & Sheen state:

> It is in this sphere of collective activities that religions in particular are likely to have to relate to the law and government administration; this is where many complaints arise over bureaucratic obstruction or failings of the state. (Boyle & Sheen, 1997, p. 7)

States are obliged to secure religious freedom, to eliminate discrimination and, as with any other right, this is dependent on "the rule of law" in a democratic society.

Lifting the Veil of Religious and Cultural Identities

Legal theorists have also made the argument that there should be a harmonisation between religious law and international human rights standards, to accept the reality of religious belief in different cultures. Restrictions placed on the right to manifest religion or belief are measures to prevent propaganda for war or the advocacy of national, racial or religious hatred.

Interestingly, freedom of religion includes the right to believe that one has exclusive truth and that what others believe is lacking in truth. However, under international standards, people should not be treated less favourably because they do not share your beliefs and, as such, differences of belief should not render you more vulnerable to discrimination. In reality, however, this is precisely what happens in many parts of the world, when discrimination and intolerance are justified by reference to the inferiority of opposing beliefs, whether religious or non-religious.

One final point on the concept of religious freedom is the right to choose and change religious commitment. International standards state clearly that there must not be coercion in matters of religion, a view shared by many faiths. It is within this right to change one's religion that people choose to convert to a religion they were not born into. With reference to Islam, for example, there have been many high profile converts to the faith. The musician Cat Stevens, now known as Yusuf Islam, has for the last few decades played an important leadership role in Britain (Parker-Jenkins 2002). Similarly, Muslim converts in Germany (Nielsen 1995) and Australia (Donohoue Clyne, 2001) have assumed a mediation role with local government and other faith groups.

Religious Identity

Having discussed the nature of religious freedom, we turn now to the concept of religious identity. The construction of identity draws on a number of factors, such as gender, sexuality and social class. Language and ethnicity are other factors which can help to give people a sense of belonging and may provide both individuals and groups collectively with a shared sense of identity. For others, there may be a religious rather than an ethnic boundary around them, a marker which helps to define their sense of self and which is a key component of their self-description. Religious identity is also connected to people's sense of feeling. People describe themselves as "feeling Jewish" or "feeling Catholic", whether they are born into the religion or have adopted it. For others, religious identity may be closely linked to religious study, especially for those in the process of converting to a faith, or it may be "all they have ever known" (Weller, Feldman, & Purdam, 2001, p. 17). When there are converts in a religious community, as noted above, it is not necessarily a shared history, but a shared religious identity, which binds people. Furthermore, religion is open to interpretation and a variety of expressions are used about what it is to be a Catholic, or what constitutes being a Muslim. In a study in Britain, Modood et al. (1997) noted that "a growing number of white people have no religious affiliation" (p. 298). This contrasted with that of South Asians groups, for example Sikhs, Hindus and Muslims, who embrace a number of religious traditions, such as Islam, Hinduism, Sikhism and Christianity. These researchers also found that "the primacy of religion in South Asian identities is owed at least partly to community relations as much as to personal faith" (p. 299).

Lifting the Veil of Religious and Cultural Identities

One of the measures of religious adherence is the frequency of attendance at places of worship. Rules governing the need to attend church, temple, synagogue or mosque vary within and among different groups. For Muslims, for example, there are also differences of opinion about whether women should worship at the mosque or in the home. Other groups, such as Hindus, often have their own private shrines at home (Oberoi, 1994; Jackson & Nesbitt, 1993). Places of worship may also be used for educational purposes, such as within supplementary education at weekends or in the evenings.

In discussing religious identity, there is not an easy way of providing categorisation, particularly because of the overlap between religion and culture. There is an assumption that race identifies faith, but this need not necessarily be true. Some people may not wish to be labelled by their ethnic background, such as "Asian Christian", but rather by their identity as a Christian, which may be what is of foremost importance to their sense of identity. The language of identity is used a great deal by group activists, as they seek to maintain their cultural heritage. Importantly, note Modood et al., "the most common expression of ethnicity is not what people do but what people say or believe about themselves" (1997, p. 332).

To summarise so far, self-description is primarily an expression of who you belong with, of membership of a community. This may extend to choice of dress or to choosing a particular religious instruction in school. The concept can also be used to provide a unifying perspective, through which we can gain a fuller and more integrated understanding of social activity or a social group.

Dimensions of Culture and Ethnicity

New cultural and religious identities are now commonplace in many parts of Europe, as a result of immigration, displacement by war and factors causing people to seek political asylum. A feature of the European landscape is the diversity of the people, characterised by place of origin, skin colour and a personal sense of identity. The importance of cultural and religious identity for some people is particularly significant and, as Young (1990) notes, it can also be a major focus of their politics. With reference to ethnic identity, Modood et al. (1997) argue that ethnic assertiveness arises out of the feeling of not being respected and a need to challenge existing power relations; not just the toleration of difference, but also questions concerning "public acknowledgement, resources and representation". This can also be applied to religious identity. Likewise, Ball et al. (2000) state that "identity is socially and culturally 'located' in time and space and inflected by rejection, displacement and desire" (p. 24).

Anthropologists have looked at the issue of difference between and within cultures and the potential for "culture clash" for those born of one ethnic background and brought up in another. In the 1970s, writers like Watson (1977), for example, described this as being caught between "two cultures". More recently, work by sociologists such as Stuart Hall (1992) point to the need to understand that cultural identity is not static. It is a dynamic process and we need to be aware of the shifting nature of new ethnicities and the dual and multiple senses of reality for some people. In Europe, there has been an increase in political activity and political consciousness among Muslims, with heated debate about the relationship between national identity, religious identity and the language of identity. Modood et al. (1997) found in their research that most second generation Caribbean and South Asians, for example, were uncomfortable with the idea of "British" being anything more than "a legal title" (p. 331). For many Muslims, and other groups, their first identity is that of religion and their national identity is secondary.

This leads us to ask the questions, are minority groups expressing themselves more politically, and is it about ethnicity, with religion as a sub-section, or, as is often the case for Muslims, is it the other way round? What is the relationship between the two? These are the sorts of questions we need to explore in order to understand the complexity of the issues concerning identity and discrimination. There are overlapping factors of identity, and we need theoretical models of understanding which are inclusive of religious, cultural, political and personal factors. Further, when we attempt to decide upon majority and minority rights, especially in the allocation of government funding, how can we accommodate different majority and minority combinations? It is important, therefore, to see that a person's identity can be constructed in terms of either religion and race or both. Hall (1992) has argued that there are new ethnicities and multiple senses of reality in evidence in the UK and in Europe (see also Lewis & Schnapper, 1994; Nielsen 1995; Werbner & Modood, 1997). On this subject, Nielsen (2000) talks of "fluid identities", or a complex of identities. Not only are identities fluid, but individuals operate, often consciously, with multiple identities, developing or selecting the one which is seen to be the most functional or useful at a particular time: what Nielsen (2000) calls "situational identity choice". So, a child in a classroom may be perceived as Muslim at school, British at home or simply an adolescent in the playground. This contradicts a common assumption among Europeans that identity is a "fixed non-moveable entity". Significantly, European institutions have tended to respond to the development of immigration and ethnic minorities with policies based on "mono-identities".

Claims of unfair treatment on the basis of religion are often made by groups that include a substantial proportion of people who also suffer discrimination on the basis of ethnicity (Weller et al, 2001). Religion and ethnicity are very complex and difficult to define or separate. Yet both are important in forming people's sense of identity. Although we may think of ethnicity in terms of colour, we are all, as Stuart Hall (1992) says, ethnically located. In a study conducted for the British government on religious discrimination in England and Wales, it was found that some religious people, as a matter of principle, make no distinction between their religion and their ethnicity or race (Weller et al.). However, within religions with a high proportion of minority ethnic group members, there is a clear overlap between religious and racial discrimination. With particular reference to Muslim communities, it was found that they "suffer from colour, racial, ethnic and religious discrimination" as "racists cannot analyse between race and religion" (Weller et al., p. 13).

The ethnic, religious and cultural aspects of people's identities often overlap and, if visibly apparent, this can lead to discrimination. Having a high profile because of one's religious or ethnic identity can make an individual more vulnerable in mainstream society, and high visibility may lead to more intense unfair treatment. In a study of Muslim women in the labour market, we found that those wishing to wear a "hijab", or head-covering, felt themselves discriminated against when seeking employment in high status professions (Parker-Jenkins, Haw, & Irving, 1997). Muslim women particularly may be more vulnerable if they wear traditional dress, whether

Lifting the Veil of Religious and Cultural Identities

worn for religious or cultural reasons. During the war on terrorism after the September 11 2001 attacks on the USA, Muslim women in North America and Europe were said to be targeted because of their religious dress *(British Muslim Survey, 2001-2)*. Being an easy target for discrimination because of choice of dress is also true of other religious groups, such as male Sikhs who wear a turban. Members of minority ethnic groups have reported that, in practice, religious and racial discrimination are not separable. As such, "where religious identities, beliefs and practices are closely linked to an individual's cultural, ethnic and national background, negative responses and unfair treatment based upon their identities and traditions may also be related to expressions of racism and xenophobia" (Weller et al., 2001, p. 15).

So, on the one hand, harassment due to religious difference may be part of an overall racist perspective and the perpetrator is targeting all of someone's vulnerabilities; on the other, religious identity is for some people the foremost aspect and expression of who they are. For example, for Muslim women and male Sikhs, the visible expressions that distinguish them as different are religious: that is, the wearing of a head covering or a turban; but they may also feel the victims of discrimination because of their ethnic origin.

We can say that some religious groups may feel that they are experiencing discrimination that leads to unfair treatment, similar to discrimination based on race, gender or disability. This can range from a violent assault to a chance remark that unintentionally conveys a preconceived idea or stereotype. It may also include treating someone unfavourably because of their religious belief, identity or practice. At institutional level, it may be the "collective failure of an organisation to provide an appropriate and professional service to people because of their religion" (Weller et al., 2001, p. 8). Examples of this might be in housing, school or employment. When considering religious issues, there is a further dimension, which can be termed as "religious disadvantage". This refers to historical privileges afforded to older, traditional churches which are not available to new, non-traditional ones. Importantly, not all unfair treatment amounts to discrimination. People may feel hurt by the views or ignorance of others with whom they come into contact, without the latter having done anything that is unlawful or discriminatory. Either way, religious discrimination may be immoral, but is not necessarily illegal. At the same time, actual discrimination may occur without there being any prejudiced views or attitudes on behalf of the individual or institution.

Cultural Discrimination

One way of decoding discrimination on the basis of religion rather than race is by using the concept of "cultural discrimination". The complexity of religious identity and ethnicity carries over into attempts to define and respond to religious discrimination. It is important to note that religious discrimination is not limited to racism or visible difference. For example, in our study of religious discrimination, one member of a Christian group observed that "the more active you are the more vulnerable you become" (Weller at al., 2001, p. 15). For some religious communities, their very existence has been and continues to be one of secrecy, because of the hostility they feel from others. As part of our research, I spoke to members of the Brethren, who reported that they choose to remain segregated, so that they can develop their religious community detached from relations with other groups or mainstream society.

Lifting the Veil of Religious and Cultural Identities

If we look at discrimination by the broader term of "cultural discrimination", then we move beyond trying to categorize exactly whether discrimination is racial or religious to recognizing the complexity of the situation. Whether or not individuals or groups feel that religion is the central issue that needs to be addressed, the wider society has its own perception and "religion is not seen as intrinsic to identity as opposed to the case where race is" (Weller et al., 2001, p. 18).

The law has been criticised for privileging "colour" within policy documents, as has the limited anti-racist policy of the 1980s, because it interprets race and racism in terms of colour only, as well as polarising the world into two groups: Black and White. In so doing, religious, political and economic differences between and within minority groups are ignored. Modood et al. (1997) argue that this has led to a narrow definition of what counts as anti-racist policy and practice in local government. The inadequacy of legislation means that the new Race Relations Act (2000) is still not broad enough to extend to cultural discrimination, despite research demonstrating that this could be a policy option: (see Weller et al. [2001, pp. 126-129] for potential new laws covering this theme). Gillborn (1995) concurs that there is bound to be a failure with this approach to connect with many minority populations whose sense of identity is based on characteristics other than race, such as religion.

Modood et al. (1997) add further that "there seems to be various forms of prejudice and discrimination which use cultural difference to vilify or marginalize or demand cultural assimilation from groups who also suffer colour racism" (p. 353). This was confirmed by our study of Muslim women in the workplace (Parker-Jenkins et al., 1997), in which we found that there was clearly a potential for people to suffer double discrimination when colour and culture overlap. Significantly, Modood et al. state that "South Asians themselves ... were more likely to identify Muslims, rather than Asians as a whole, as the group against whom there is most hostility" (p. 353). Such anti-Muslim prejudice is seen as "a White reaction to the revival of Islamic self-confidence and self-assertion in Britain and elsewhere" (p. 353).

Theorists stress the need to challenge general assumptions underpinning anti-racist policy. Gilroy (1987) examines shifting notions of race, nation and power, and the failure of government to articulate anti-racism in a manner which is not only inclusive, but which also has the ability to attack "new racism". He calls for more theoretical and dynamic understanding of race and racism. Echoing Giroux's (1991) view that there are no fixed boundaries, Gilroy maintains that "the culture which defines the groups we know as races is never fixed, finished or final. It is fluid, it is actively and continually made and re-made" (1990, p. 80).

In challenging existing paradigms or models of identity, therefore, we need to be aware of broader and more dynamic concepts of ethnicity. Modood (1989, p. 284) argues persuasively that

> Neither Muslims nor any other religious-ethnic minorities will be understood unless current race philosophies are re-evaluated. The beginning of that understanding is the appreciation of the centrality of religion to the Muslim and perhaps also to the Sikh and Hindu psyche: that it is of far more importance and central to self-definition than "race" or than can be allowed for by the Black-White view of the world.

Lifting the Veil of Religious and Cultural Identities

It is also the case that, for many in society, life is secular and they do not themselves have a religious identity. Conversely, others reject the idea that religious obligations can be negotiated in school and at work, and in some way traded off; that you can choose to live without religious belief, or parts of it, and not change what you are, but change what you do at certain times.

Research suggests that the identities of young people within minority ethnic communities are more hybrid than those of their parents or grandparents (Hall, 1992; Gillborn, 1995; Modood et al., 1997). There is also a view that religious identity will diminish in forthcoming generations, especially among minority ethnic groups (Sarwar, 1994). Certainly, adolescence is a time when young people wish to belong with their peers and may therefore pull away from their religion, seeking out alternative ways of belonging. Yet, in Britain and France, for example, we also see cases of young people being more politically aware and being prepared to stand up for their religious rights. The wearing of a "hijab", or headscarf, is not compromised by girls at school today, whereas previous generations were denied access to schooling because of this choice of dress (Parker-Jenkins, 1995). Older generations were prepared to accept situations as part of the prevailing ideology of assimilation and integration in the 1950s that new generations may not. A move away from becoming more "Westernised" to one of becoming politicised about one's culture and identity is evident, especially among Muslim communities (Parker-Jenkins, 2002).

Is there bound to be discrimination against people who are different? Is there also a likelihood that there will be resentment of new people coming into an area, whether they are perceived to be religious or not? Is it that people do not like change and fear things which appear different or foreign, not of our country or area? Is this natural among humans or a sign of insecurity? Choices in school, for example, are, as Ball et al. (2000) state, "bound up with the expression and suppression of identities" (p.24). Is religious identity a source of constraint upon pupils'/students' choices at school and, later, at work? There are no easy answers, but teachers especially need to be aware of this vulnerability and the potential for children to suffer discrimination due to racism or religious bigotry. An awareness of difference, and the ways in which schools can accommodate religious obligations, are some of the implications that needs to inform policy for initial and in-service teacher education. In addressing these issues, teachers are now able through new curriculum directives to explore the potential for "citizenship" to have a more inclusive definition.

Identity and Citizenship

Since 1945, the stability and self-assurance which countries previously felt have been deeply challenged by immigration and the position of minority ethnic groups in the West and by the disappearance of communism in the East. There remains a range of unresolved conflicts from a previous era in which nationality, culture, religion and citizenship are again being contested.

The concept of citizenship has different legal meanings across the world. Throughout Europe, for example, legislation has been passed denoting a person's status in the country. There are legal traditions which give preference to those born within the territory of a state (for example, Britain) and therefore citizenship is extended to the children of immigrants. Alternatively, some countries pass on citizenship by descent. Nielsen (1995) states that "Germany has always insisted that it is not a country of immigration, so the term 'guest worker' remains in common usage" (p. 25). Owing to the lack of full citizenship, there are limitations with regard to access to welfare benefits and the ability to participate in the political process. The question arises as to whether or not German citizenship can be extended to Turks within the context of dual nationality, as in Switzerland and Canada. With the change of government in Germany in 1998, for example, the concept of dual citizenship has been placed on the political agenda. Nielsen argues that "immigration law has been used in various ways to limit access to full citizenship by the simple expedient of keeping people out or letting them in under conditions which exclude them from access to naturalisation" (p. 25). Moreover, in many European countries the ability to participate in the political process is dependent on citizenship, particularly at national level.

During the last few decades, Britain has had to come to terms with the reality of being a multi-cultural, multi-lingual and multi-faith society. The same is true of other European states, such as Denmark, which is struggling to construct a positive national identity among children from diverse backgrounds (*The Times Educational Supplement*, 2002, November 15). This issue is about accommodating new realities, among them cultural, ethnic and religious pluralism. It also involves practical and symbolic measures and, as Nielsen (1995) suggests, a continuing development of what we mean by nationality, which is changing the definitions of "us" and "them" (Said, 1978) and signifying a discernable shift whereby "the outsider is moving inside" (Nielsen, 1995, p. 26).

It is the ability of European national identity at this level to shift and show flexibility which will determine the extent to which minorities will allow themselves to be integrated and to become European, for "the law can in both its content and in its practice be welcoming or excluding of newcomers" (Nielsen, 1995, p. 9).

The introduction of "Citizenship" into the National Curriculum in the academic year 2002-3 provides a powerful opportunity for all schools to enrich teaching with a subject directly related to the future lives of young people. Within the "Citizenship" Framework, there are a number of key areas which can be easily used by schools of all kinds to promote peace and social justice. In terms of the specific question, "How do we promote peace and justice in schools?", the curriculum area of citizenship could be a natural choice. We need, however, to define closely what we mean by "peace", and "justice"; the various ways in which we can interpret these terms; and, most importantly, we need to ask who "we" are? The perspectives of a range of different communities (regional, national and global) should be included, particularly in the light of seriously distorted images conveyed by some sections of the media in the aftermath of the September 11th bombings. There is a danger that we see terrorism as a "Muslim issue", when in fact bombings go back several decades and have been committed by different groups, as evidenced in Ireland and the Middle East.

We need to open up debate and provide a selection of references regarding citizenship. The choice of language, such as "fundamentalism" and "xenophobia", also needs to form part of this analysis. In attempting to obtain and enter into an alternative point of view, such as that based on Islam or Judaism, evidence may be found through sources in the community and teaching texts beyond those produced by British-American publishers. In the same way that we talked about the dangers inherent in transmitting ethno-centric, Brito-centric and Euro-centric perspectives when the National Curriculum was first introduced by the Education Reform Act 1988, we need to continue exploring different sources and different points of view. Community schools will no doubt engage in such discussions at a general level; faith schools will need to look at other religions and culturally different groups to open up debate. No school can claim to be totally neutral and many minority religious groups feel that state schools promote a White, middle-class, Christian point of view (Parker-Jenkins 1995). Clearly, it is not easy for schools to handle controversial issues such as peace and justice, but what is the alternative? (McLaughlin, 2002).

It is also a mistake to believe that the concept of "citizenship" sits in isolation from other curriculum areas. A cross-curricular approach to teaching it, in English and History, for example, should be developed within schools. We know from the 1980s and 1990s that teaching multi-culturalism and anti-racism as discrete aspects of the school curriculum ensured their marginalisation. This was particularly true if they formed no part of the assessment process. The concept of citizenship needs to be imbedded in the formal curriculum and informally, in other appropriate ways, in order to secure its importance in the school. Through the character of the school, its organisation and rituals, and through the teacher as role model, a multi-dimensional approach can be used to promote the concept. The role of OFSTED will also be important in supporting teachers to develop dialogue and disseminate good practice in this evolving part of the curriculum. Teachers will have to deal with complicated issues surrounding citizenship and they will have to think about the subject in the broadest sense. In that regard, it is important to provide support both within and beyond the school.

Using "Citizenship" in the National Curriculum as a vehicle for cross-cultural dialogue, there are therefore a range of strategies schools could use in challenging discrimination and prejudice. Joint sports and cultural events, exchange programmes for staff and pupils, and "twinning" schools with those of a different religious background, are possibilities. I advocated this in 1995 within the context of accommodating Muslim children's educational needs and the idea has been established more recently within a number of schemes. Gloucestershire University's AMSCITT Scheme, 1999-2002, for example, was based on training Muslim teachers by giving them a "twinning" experience in Muslim and non-Muslim schools (Parker-Jenkins, 2002). Such efforts clearly allow the opportunity for negative stereotypes on both sides to be challenged.

It would be wrong to assume that responsibility for dealing with issues of discrimination and prejudice rests only with minority communities and/or faith schools. Riots in the Northern towns of England demonstrated very clearly that young people educated predominantly in community schools were articulating hostility and hatred. Ignorance, misunderstanding and unemployment were said to be at the centre of unrest, made worse by policy at local government level, which has done little to change the pattern of social segregation. For example, it was said that:

> There are a small number of deprived estates where White children have never made an Asian friend and vice versa..... For many people, the first prolonged contact with different cultures comes at sixth-form college. By then, isolation, poverty and unemployment have already cemented attitudes on race. (*The Guardian*, 2002, December 12, p. 5)

Lifting the Veil of Religious and Cultural Identities

Reports into the riots in Oldham, Burnley and Bradford in 2001 stated that segregation has left many communities marginalised. Significantly, it was also stated that regeneration funding should be available, not only for minority ethnic group needs, but for other groups, in order to avoid inter-community envy (*The Times Higher Education Supplement,* 2001, December 14). This was because among the perpetrators there were high numbers of unemployed White youths. Also at issue was the extent to which many people in the region had retreated behind ethnic lines; this was exacerbated by segregated schooling and housing.

Of the 70-plus recommendations from the reports into the disturbances, a national debate on the concept of "citizenship" was suggested and this has involved the question of taking an oath of allegiance. The question arises of whether or not a Muslim, for example, should "insist that his religio-cultural priorities ...override his civic duties of loyalty, tolerance, justice and respect for democracy?" (*The Times Education Supplement,* 2002, January 18, p. 7). Similarly, in the "loyalty debate", David Blunkett has put forward the idea of a scheme for new immigrant education in citizenship. (This is a practice in Canada, for example). These debates raise the questions, "What does it means to be a British citizen in Britain and in a global world?"; "How would disloyalty be construed?"; and "Who would decide?". This issue of identity and belonging emerged in a study I conducted in a Muslim girls' school, when one girl said, "In this country we're always Asian, never British!" (Parker-Jenkins & Haw, 1996). The continued notion of immigrant, non-British status within that of the wider community is false. Given that these young people are British, we need to allow for a personal sense of identity, which includes their ethnic, national, regional and religious backgrounds. For children particularly, there are not only dual, but also multiple, senses of reality and they negotiate their way around a number of different social contexts and membership groups at school, home and society in general.

The "depth of polarisation" between communities which rarely overlap is one of the key issues emerging from inquiries into social unrest in Britain. It is argued that the intended expansion of faith schools will serve to fuel tensions by reinforcing the polarisation of a mono-cultural educational experience in segregated communities, rather than opening up school communities, pulling down barriers and helping to dispel negative stereotyping (Parker-Jenkins, Hartas, & Irving, 2004). There are no easy answers to problems of racism and religious bigotry, and local communities themselves will have to become centrally involved. This was underscored by the head teacher of Oldham Church of England Secondary School, which received a lot of media attention during the riots, who said, "We are perceived as being part of the problem in Oldham. We want to be part of the solution", (*The Times Educational Supplement*, 2002, January 18, p. 7). As part of this response, the school has looked to change its admissions policy, and 15% of its intake will now be from other than Christian denominations. There have also been calls to close all faith schools, and pursue a policy of desegregation (Parker-Jenkins, 2002). A common school for all has appeal, but desegregation is unlikely to be realistic in areas within the Home Counties or Bradford.

Despite their mono-faith composition, it is of course the fact that some faith schools are representative of a wide range of nationalities and cultures. The Islamia Primary School, for example, has 23 different nationalities represented, some non-Muslim staff, and an admissions policy open to those of all faiths (Treverne, 2002). It is argued that a great deal has been done by faith schools and community schools to break down barriers, and that a mono-cultural profile is the result of demographics. Conversely, in some cases there is little diversity in some faith schools. This is said to be due to the conservative/orthodox element within some religious traditions that avoid "outreach" to other communities. Similarly, some community schools in parts of Britain, like Cambridgeshire, have little diversity, due to demographic patterns. At Key Stage 3 and 4 of the National Curriculum, there is now a requirement that all children have knowledge and understanding of the religious diversity in the country, making it more difficult for state-maintained schools to countenance a single-faith/mono-cultural perspective within teaching.

It is right to have open debate about problems between different communities, but what has not been openly acknowledged is the issue of "parallel lives" lived by communities in the same geographical area and reinforced by patterns of schooling. The Committee of Inquiry into the Education of Children from Ethnic Minority Groups [Swann] Report (1985) and the Macpherson Report (1999), for example, highlighted issues of ethnicity, socio-economic class, underachievement and a sense of belonging. The question is, "How far can schools go in acknowledging religious beliefs, and do they have an obligation to foster social cohesion?" Whilst issues concerning legislative reform and racial tensions may lie outside the control of schools, they do have a role to play in reducing barriers of prejudice and developing a shared notion of citizenship. What is needed is a common sense of belonging and co-operation, with groups and potentially coalitions of different religious and non-religious groups working together to effect change. Importantly, there is a need for Muslims themselves, and those who feel particularly discriminated against, to engage in all levels of society, to avoid others, however well-meaning, speaking for them and attempting to give them a "voice".

Conclusion

The right to religious freedom is supported by legal documents at national and international level and this provides protection for those of a religious background, as well as those who do not profess any religious belief. However, in reality, if we define discrimination on the basis of religion, there are many instances when people do not enjoy this religious freedom and they face prejudice and discrimination. The concept of identity draws upon a number of factors, but religion particularly is a significant marker for many individuals or groups; so much so that they are willing to become politically active to challenge what they see as unfair treatment by individuals, institutions or the state. Economic changes in Europe in the post-1945 period has caused a huge number of people to leave their own country and take up work elsewhere, and part of this diaspora brought with it new religions to Western Europe, such as Islam, Sikhism and Hinduism. Consequently, there has been a substantial growth of religious communities in many European states, consisting of groups looking for economic prosperity and also wishing to maintain their religious and cultural heritage. There are practical ways at international level to enhance freedom of thought, religion and belief, but there is also a need for commitment from individual nations to protect religious freedom and to challenge racism, hatred of "foreigners", and xenophobia. In many countries, such as the former Yugoslavia, it is difficult to isolate what is religious prejudice from intolerance inspired by racist, ethnic or nationalistic feelings. The common core of policy to tackle these prejudices has to be an education that leads to the acceptance of equality and diversity with respect to beliefs. As part of this debate, we need to consider what constitutes citizenship in multi-cultural/multi-lingual/multi-faith societies, and the extent to which citizenship is made problematic by religious identity.

In the light of the terrorist attacks of September 11th, the issue of citizenship has emerged as a central concern of political debates today, and particularly the core values upon which citizenship within a modern state should be based. Inquiries into the 2001 riots in the North of England concluded that "a meaningful concept of citizenship", which recognises the contributions of all cultures to Britain's development and prosperity, needs to be developed. Given the developing notion of "Citizenship" in the UK National Curricula and the pro-equity initiatives that are part of the European Union agenda, it is timely to consider how these can be expressed in faith schools and others. Despite evidence of secularisation in our society, religion remains a significant individual and social force, which can cause people to divide, as demonstrated so clearly in national and global events. However, given that the definition of education means to lead out of ignorance, schools particularly are in an ideal position to reflect on what needs to be done on a number of fronts, to ensure a truly broad and balanced curriculum for those young people who will ultimately be responsible for us all in the future.

References

Ball, S. J., Maguire, M., & Macrae, S. (Eds.) (2000). *Choice, pathways and transitions post-16: New youth, new economies in the global city.* London: RoutledgeFalmer.

Barker, E. (1989). *New religious movements: A practical introduction*. London: HMSO.

Barrett, D. V. (1996). *Sects, "cults" and alternative religions: A world survey and sourcebook*. London: Blandford.

Bowker, J. (Ed.) (1997). *The Oxford dictionary of world religions*. Oxford: Oxford University Press.

Boyle, K., & Sheen, J. (Eds.) (1997). *Freedom of religion and belief: A world report*. London: Routledge.

British Muslims: Monthly Survey. (2001-02). Birmingham: Centre for the Study of Islam and Christian-Muslim Relations.

Committee of Inquiry into the Education of Children from Ethnic Minority Groups (1985). *Education for all*. London: HMSO.

Council of Europe (1950). *Convention for the protection of human rights and fundamental freedoms*. Strasbourg: Author.

Coward, H., Hinnells, J. R., & Williams, R. B. (Eds.) (2000). *The South Asian religious diaspora in Britain, Canada, and the United States*. Albany, NY: State University of New York Press.

Donohoue Clyne, I. (2001). Educating Muslim children in Australia. In A. Saeed & S. Akbarzadeh, (Eds.), *Muslim*

Lifting the Veil of Religious and Cultural Identities

communities in Australia (pp. 116-137). Sydney: University of New South Wales Press.

Education Reform Act: Elizabeth II, 1988, Chapter 40 (1988). London: HMSO.

Gillborn, D. (1995). *Racism & antiracism in real schools: Theory, policy, practice.* Buckingham: Open University Press.

Gilroy, P. (1987). *"There ain't no black in the Union Jack": The cultural politics of race and nation.* London: Hutchinson.

Gilroy, P. (1990). The end of anti-racism. *New Community, 17,* 71-83.

Giroux, H. A. (1991). Postmodernism and the discourse of educational criticism. In S. Aronowitz & H. A. Giroux, *Postmodern education: Politics, culture, and social criticism.* Minneapolis: University of Minnesota Press.

The Guardian (2002, December 12). Article, p. 5.

Hall, S. (1992). New ethnicities. In J. Donald & A. Rattansi, (Eds.), *'Race', culture and difference* (pp. 252-259). London: Sage Publications.

Hinnells, J. R. (Ed.) (1997). *A new handbook of living religions.* Oxford: Blackwell Publishers.

Humanist Philosophers' Group. (2001). *Religious schools: The case against.* London: British Humanist Association.

Jackson, R., & Nesbitt, E. (1993). *Hindu children in Britain.* Stoke-on-Trent: Trentham.

Lewis, B., & Schnapper, D. (Eds.) (1994). *Muslims in Europe.* London: Pinter.

Lewis, P, (1994). *Islamic Britain: Religion, politics and identity among British Muslims: Bradford in the 1990s.* London: I.B.Taurus.

Macpherson, W. (1999). *The Stephen Lawrence inquiry.* London: Stationery Office.

McLaughlin, T. H. (2002, October). Paper presented at the Seminar for Peace and Justice in the Light of September 11th, Homerton College, University of Cambridge.

Modood, T. (1989). Religious anger and minority rights. *The Political Quarterly, 60,* 280-284.

Modood, T., Berthoud, R., Lakey, J., Nazroo, J., Smith, P., Virdec, S., et al. (1997). *Ethnic minorities in Britain: Diversity and disadvantage: The fourth national survey of ethnic minorities.* London: Policy Studies Institute.

Nielsen, J. S. (1995). *Muslims in Western Europe.* (2nd ed.) Edinburgh: Edinburgh University Press.

Nielsen, J. S. (2000). Fluid identities: Muslims and Western Europe's nation states. *Cambridge Review of International Affairs, 13* (2), 212-217.

Oberoi, H. (1994). *The construction of religious boundaries: Culture, identity and diversity in the Sikh tradition.* Delhi: Oxford University Press.

Parker-Jenkins, M. (1995). *Children of Islam : A teacher's guide to meeting the needs of Muslim pupils.* Stoke-on-Trent: Trentham Books.

Parker-Jenkins, M. (2002). Equal access to state schools: The case of Muslim schools in Britain. *Race, Ethnicity and Education, 5* (3), 273-289.

Parker-Jenkins, M., Hartas, D, & Irving B. A. (2004). *In good faith: Schools, religion, and public funding.* Aldershot: Ashgate.

Parker-Jenkins, M., & Haw, K. F. (1996). Equality within Islam, not without it: The perspectives of Muslim girls in a Muslim school in Britain. *Muslim Educational Quarterly, 3 (3),* 17-34.

(A report of findings from an ESRC funded project).

Parker-Jenkins, M., Haw, K. F., & Irving, B. (1997). Social inclusion and career opportunities: The experience of Muslim women. *The European Educational Research Journal.*

(A report of findings from a Leverhulme Trust funded project).

Race Relations (Amendment) Act: Elizabeth II, 2000, Chapter 34 (2000). London: Stationery Office.

Said, E. W. (1978). *Orientalism*. New York: Pantheon Books.

Sarwar, G. (1994). *British Muslims and schools*. London: Muslim Educational Trust.

Smart, N. (1989). *The world's religions: Old traditions and modern transformations*. Cambridge: Cambridge University Press.

The Times Educational Supplement (2002, January 18). Article (p. 7).

The Times Educational Supplement (2002, November 15). Countries come to terms with their identity crises, by D. Hofkins (p. 23).

The Times Higher Education Supplement (2001, December 14). Article (p. 30).

Treverne, A. (2002, May). Paper presented at the Seminar "Faith Schools after Bradford".

UK Department for Education and Skills, Qualifications and Curriculum Authority. (2001). *Citizenship: A scheme of work for Key Stage 3*. London: Author.

UK Department for Education and Skills, Qualifications and Curriculum Authority. (2002). *Citizenship: A scheme of work for Key Stage 4*. London: Author.

United Nations (1981). Universal declaration of human rights. In I. Brownlie (Ed.), *Basic documents on human rights*. Oxford: Clarendon Press. (Original work published 1948).

United Nations (1989). *Convention on the rights of the child*. New York: Author.

Watson, J. L. (Ed.) (1977). *Between two cultures: Migrants and minorities in Britain*. Oxford: Basil Blackwell.

Weller, P., Feldman, A., & Purdam, K. (2001). *Religious discrimination in England and Wales*. London: Home Office.

Werbner, P., & Modood, T. (Eds.) (1997). *Debating cultural hybridity: Multi-cultural identities and the politics of anti-racism*. London: Zed Books.

Young, I. M. (1990). *Justice and the politics of difference*. Princeton, NJ: Princeton University Press.

Additional Reading

Abdullah, M. S. (1981). *Geschichte des Islams in Deutschland*. Graz: Styria.

Baumann, G. (1996). *Contesting cultures: Discourses of identity in multi-ethnic London.* Cambridge: Cambridge University Press.

Bina, C. (1996). Toward a new world order: US hegemony, client-states and Islamic alternative. In Hussin Mutalib, & Hashmi, T. u-I. (Eds.), *Islam, Muslims and the modern state: Case-studies of Muslims in thirteen countries* (pp. 3-30). Basingstoke: Macmillan.

Church Schools Review Group. (2001). The way ahead: Church of England schools in the new millennium. London: Church House Publishing.

Education Guardian (2002, September 3). Being sociable: Will Woodward meets pupils and teachers starting their compulsory citizenship lessons, by W. Woodward (pp. 2-3)

Education Guardian (2002, September 17). Art of living earns its slot, by P. Revell (p. 3).

Hussin Mutalib, & Hashni, T. u-I. (Eds.) (1994). *Islam, Muslims and the modern state: Case-studies of Muslims in thirteen countries.* Basingstoke: Macmillan.

Sacks, J. (1997). *The politics of hope.* London: Jonathan Cape.

Said, E. W. (1997) *Covering Islam: How the media and the experts determine how we see the rest of the world.* (Rev. ed.) London: Vintage Books.

Shadid, W. A. R., & Koningsveld, P. S. van (Eds.) (1996). *Muslims in the margin: Political responses to the presence of Islam in Western Europe.* Kampen, Netherlands: Kok Pharos.

The Times Educational Supplement (2001, November 30). Faith facts (p. 7).

The Times Educational Supplement (2002, December 5). Blunkett faces religious wrath (p. 4).

UK Department for Education and Employment. (2001). *Schools: Building on success: Raising standards, promoting diversity, achieving results.* London: Stationery Office.

Werbner, P. (2002). *Imagined diasporas among Manchester Muslims: The public performance of Pakistani transnational identity politics.* Oxford: James Currey.

Yuval-Davis, N. (1992). Fundamentalism, multiculturalism and women in Britain. In J. Donald & A. Rattansi (Eds.), *"Race", culture and difference* (pp. 278-293). London: Sage Publications.

2

GROWING OLD INVISIBLY: OLDER VIEWERS TALK TELEVISION[1]

Tim Healey and Karen Ross

Throughout the developed world, people are living longer and having fewer children, so that the population balance is changing rapidly: by 2020, every other person in Europe will be 50+ and in Britain 11.8 million adults will be of a pensionable age by 2010 (*Labour Market Trends,* 1998). In an environment in which being an older person[2] is becoming a more common experience, how is it that, instead of dealing with this changing social, economic and cultural dynamic, the mass medium of television seems largely youth orientated? Analysing the way(s) in which older people are portrayed on our TV screens has been a source of academic research since the popularisation of TV in the United States in the 1950s. Whilst media investigations of age/ing and its portrayal have been far less prolific than, say, studies of ethnicity or gender, there have nonetheless been a steady stream of studies, mostly in the USA and

---

[1] This chapter was originally published in article form in *Media, Culture & Society,* 24 (1), 2002, pp. 105-120, © Sage Publications, and we are grateful to Sage Publications for their permission to reprint the article here. It was presented as a paper at Chester by Karen Ross.
[2] For the purposes of this essay, the term "older" is taken to mean "over 50 years", in line with Age Concern England's common definition.

often focused on the dissonance between the proportion of the population who were "older" people and their corresponding visibility across the television landscape. Most of these studies were carried out in the 1970s, when interest in content analysis was particularly popular (see Petersen, 1973; Aronoff, 1974; Northcote, 1975; Harris & Feinberg, 1977; Ansello, 1978), although more recent studies carried out in Britain (Communications Research Group, 1999; Hanley, 2000; Healey & Ross, 2002) have come to remarkably similar conclusions. Robinson and Skill (1995, p. 385), noting the lack of authoritative studies since the 1970s, concluded as a result of their own work that:

> Overall, very little had changed. The implications of these findings, however, are quite significant. The elderly continue to be infrequently seen on television and when they do appear, they occupy lead roles at about one half of the rate of other age groups.

Compared to the more recent British work, the finding cited above of 50% under-representation of older people in lead roles is highly positive. A publication from Age Concern England, for example, concluded that, while older people comprise 21% of the real world population in Britain, they only populate 7% of the TV world, and older men feature more than twice as often as older women, neatly reversing the real, lived experience (Communications Research Group, 1999). Whilst this mismatch between "TVworld" and "Realworld" is hardly a novel finding and much research work which has focused on other kinds of demographics, such as race, gender and disability, have found the same kinds of contradictions (see Cumberbatch & Negrine, 1992; Ross 1997; Bourne 1998), it nonetheless remains troubling. It is troubling because, although the idea that TV is merely a window on the world has never been taken completely seriously, the past decade does seem to have witnessed a step-change in the contours of television's socio-cultural map. A paradox seems to be emerging. On the one hand, globalisation, media conglomeratisation and the ICT explosion give us (or at least those of us in the developed world who enjoy cheap and accessible media services) unparalleled access to a rich diversity of programmes and genres; but, at the same time, the actual content, at least of mainstream, prime-time TV, appears to reflect an identikit world of young/ish people, mostly white, mostly heterosexual, mostly obeying conventional social norms. It is not surprising, then, that studies of viewer perceptions (see Broadcasting Standards Council, 1994; 1995) conclude that, in the main, people are not satisfied with the viewing choices offered to them and do not see themselves reflected in television's golden glow.

Whilst much of the debate around portrayal issues has been oriented towards studies which take a content analytic approach, rather fewer researchers carry out work with the consumers of media outputs. This is partly because of the pragmatic reason that audience research is both costly and extremely time intensive, but also for philosophical and ideological reasons, inasmuch as it became deeply unfashionable to think of consumers as members of a group called "the audience". However, in the past few years there has been a resurgence in the ways in which media scholars now conceptualise the viewers, listeners and readers of mass media and, once again, "the audience" is back on the agenda as a legitimate locus for research. But, of course, most interest has been shown in those audiences which share a defining characteristic, such as gender, ethnicity or disability, since much of the impetus for such studies has come from the media industry itself and its desire to retain or, preferably, capture market share as a consequence of a better understanding of what the customer wants (Kent, 1994; Healey & Ross, 2002). It is a little odd, then, that interest in that most loyal of audience groups, the older consumer, has not been seen as an important segment for the industry to interrogate, although perhaps not so odd if we understand the heavy thread that binds advertising and television together: advertisers are not interested in the older market and therefore media organisations work much harder at trying to attract younger audiences, which they can then deliver up to advertisers in return for serious money. The work on which this paper is based, therefore, represents a significant and timely intervention in the broad arena of contemporary audience studies and attempts to offer some insights into the ways in which older media users react to and interact with the medium of television.

The Effect of Affect: a Case Study of Older Viewers

In early 2000, the commercial British broadcaster Carlton TV and its sister company, Ondigital, commissioned one of the authors of this paper (Karen Ross) to undertake a research project with older viewers, in an effort to understand better a significant part of their traditional audience (for Carlton) and the interest that older people might have in taking up digital services (for Ondigital). Broadly, the study aimed to identify what viewers thought about the ways in which older age is portrayed and how themes of age and ageing are treated on television. It also intended to explore the viability of themed broadcasting targeted at older audiences, either as a separate channel possibly delivered as a digital service or as a strand of mainstream programming delivered via the existing terrestrial TV network. The study's secondary aim was to ascertain knowledge about, and interest in, alternative and additional broadcast services, such as cable, satellite and digital, in order to determine if older people were a potential source of new subscribers to Ondigital's products.

The University team worked with an existing network of older advocates to identify the study's sample base and, using snowball techniques, 24 focus groups were organised across the nations and regions of Britain and Northern Ireland, each with an older person as facilitator. Because of the low market penetration of digital services generally across the UK, it was decided to organise a further four groups of known Ondigital subscribers to interview, so as to gather market intelligence on what individuals liked and disliked about the service. These latter groups were asked the same questions as the others, and their responses differed from the "mainstream" groups only insofar as they obviously had much more knowledge about multi-channel systems and had a much wider range of programmes from which to select their viewing choices. In all other respects, though, the same themes emerged from these groups as the others, so, for the purposes of this essay, the responses from all the groups will be considered together: a total of 228 people eventually participated in the study. We are well aware of the problems which such a method provokes, not least a blurring of the subtle (and sometimes quite overt) differences between individuals, forcing a flattening out and homogenising of perspectives, which disavows precisely the creative autonomy which in other circumstances we would be keen to champion. However, the potential to explore those nuanced positions is the inevitable casualty of trying to combine the richness of an interview-based approach with an industry-led demand for a large sample size. Despite the limitations of the method, though, the repetitive articulation of the same themes across the great majority of the groups encourages us to believe that our findings nonetheless provide important and meaningful insights into the ways in which older viewers regard the portrayal of older age. Whilst there was often disagreement within groups about the meaning and/or pleasures of particular characterisations, there was considerable accord around specific themes, which are explored in more detail below.

As well as taking part in the interviews, participants also completed a short questionnaire, which we used to gather broad-based quantitative data about programme preferences and interest in a range of interactive broadcast services which are available via digital technology, such as shopping online, enhanced programming, e-mail and the Internet. We were keen to ensure that the sample comprised "ordinary" people, rather than individuals who had specialist knowledge of or interest in broadcasting (notwithstanding the purposive sample of Ondigital subscribers who were included), in order that the findings could be better generalised to a wider population. The use of older people's friendship groups, local community networks, membership of luncheon clubs and other recreational facilities resulted in participants being drawn from a diverse social, economic and cultural background, in which the principal characteristics which they shared, often in the absence of any other, was their self-description of being an "older person" and an interest and desire to talk about television.

Sex'n'Drugs'n'Rock'n'Roll

Whilst the study's principal focus was on images of older age, we began the interviews by asking people for their views on TV programmes generally and, in this preliminary part of the discussion, the single most frequently mentioned issue was the ubiquity of swearing. Not only did they feel personally assaulted by the constancy of swearing across many entertainment genres but, as importantly, they felt embarrassed to view TV programmes in a family environment. This mirrors results from the work of Hanley (2000), who asserts that older viewers were concerned about standards in respect of content because they suspect explicit sex, gratuitous violence and bad language are being used cynically by the programmers to attract audiences. This was particularly the case for viewers who spend a lot of time with their grandchildren or who live with an adult daughter or son. As with other elements of the TV diet which older audiences dislike, such as the prevalence of sex and violence across mainstream broadcasting, the pervasive presence of swearing in dramas, soaps and comedy was seen as a response to the media's constant search for the youth market, for whom swearing, from the point of view of older people, "just comes naturally".

> I think that television at the moment reflects the society we live in, but I'm certainly not used to the language which is used, swearing and all those 'F' words. But it's in common usage, not just among the workmen, but among educated people as well and this irritates me. (Jenny, London)[3]

---

[3] All the names have been changed.

Growing Old Invisibly

> When Rhett Butler took Scarlett O'Hara to the bedroom and kicked the door shut, we all knew what was going on; we didn't need to see a blow-by-blow account. (Fred, Belfast)

In the context of planning programmes which older people want and would enjoy, we asked viewers if they believe that broadcasters think that they are an important audience to cultivate. In the group discussions, absolutely no one did believe that broadcasters gave a moment's thought to their concerns or interests.

> They think if you're old, you just sit at home and watch the television. (Elsie, Watford)

> You're not important any more, you're finished!! (Sarah, Coventry)

> We don't really count, we're just something that happens to be around. (Brian, Darlington)

A number of viewers suggested that it was easy to see exactly what programme makers think of them as a specific audience by the kinds of programmes they put on when they assume they have a large number of older people watching: "They put on any old dross in the afternoons because they think we're too stupid to notice". Viewers point out that the kinds of advertisements that are broadcast during late mornings and early afternoons are often for products and services such as retirement homes, stairlifts and incontinence aids, which are obviously targeted at older consumers. This was seen by viewers as not only grossly patronising, but commercially stupid.

Decoding Discrimination

> They [the advertisers] are commercially naïve, because I have a much higher level of disposable income than many younger people, but I don't want to know about pension plans and conservatories; it's embarrassing and patronising. I'm just as interested in buying a Ford Focus as a younger guy. (Charlie, Bromley)

The Tropes of Older Age

The way in which programmes and advertising include a very narrow repertoire of images of older people not only has implications for commerce, but, as Davis & Davis (1985, p. 54) point out in their review of TV's images of age, the negative portrayals of older people impact on the ways in which older people are perceived by the community at large: " ... nowhere might that image projection be more damaging than in commercials. Here is where promises are made. That one can buy youth, or at least youthful appearance, endows that state and quality with high value".

A series of consistent themes emerged from the groups and they were very clear about the numerous negative ways in which older people are portrayed on TV. The concept of negative stereotyping was repeated, in different ways, in all the group discussions and can be broadly summarised as: dependent, frail, vulnerable, poor, worthless, asexual, isolated, grumpy, behind the times, stupid, miserable, gaga, pathetic and a drain on society.

It should be said, however, that a few viewers did not believe that there *was* a problem with the portrayal of older age on TV, or at least felt that what is broadcast now is much better than it used to be; but across the focus groups this was very much a minority perception.

> I don't really see it as an issue. There's such a vast range of programmes, obviously there's going to be some programmes where older people are portrayed in a negative way, but then there are other programmes that make up for it. (Bob, London)

> There's always this pathetic element, but older people have lived through this twentieth century, they have such a wealth of experience and society doesn't put any value on it. It doesn't chime with society, so you wouldn't expect it to be seen on TV, but actually the media could change that attitude because it's just not valid. (Ruth, Stirling)

This tension reflects the unclear picture which has emerged from other published research. Summarising studies mostly carried out in the USA and conducted during the 1970s, Robinson & Skill (1995) suggest that most older characters in mainstream shows had minor roles, were unlikely to have a positive love relationship and were likely to be living alone, were more likely to portray comic roles, were often portrayed as foolish and eccentric, were not treated with courtesy and respect, lacked common sense and often "acted silly" (especially women). In contrast, other research during the same period found that older people were not generally portrayed as senile, were no more likely to live alone than other characters, were not institutionalised and no more likely to live in poverty

(Northcote 1975). Dail (1988) concluded that portrayals of older people on US television *had* improved, largely in response to an ageing population which had, and has, considerable political and economic power. Robinson & Skill (1995) note that very little research actually took place during much of the 1990s in the USA to track the ways in which older people have been portrayed in recent times. Their own research, seeking to address this gap, found that, in fact, very little *had* changed. Older people are typically cast in supporting roles – roles which Robinson & Skill's "peripheral imagery" theory suggests are necessarily portrayed in stereotypical terms.

Triumphs and Tragedies: Contradictions in Readings

Most participants in our study cited a particular character or several characters who they believe provide very poor representations of older age, displaying one or more of the above characteristics. But the issue is less about always being "positive" about older people than about showing the diversity of older people's lives and experiences. Often, single plays and dramas were identified as being the worst "culprits" in their stereotypical portraits of older age, with viewers suggesting that older people are often placed in these narratives to provoke a sympathy vote (frail old person as victim or lonely); they rarely feature as a strong leading character (with the exception of detective shows, which often do feature an older man, but where older women are mostly invisible). There was a recognition that, in some genres, the dramatic convention requires an element of typecasting and older characters are just as vulnerable to such caricature as any other "type" of character, although, as with their views on other shows, there were fundamental differences in perceptions amongst audiences in this study. Conflicting views about the positive or negative nature of particular characterisations were most marked in discussions around situation comedies, such as *One Foot in the Grave* and *Last of the Summer Wine*, with both women and men having strong views on the nature of Victor Meldrew, the permanently enraged character played by the Scottish actor Richard Wilson, and its potential impact on wider society, as well as on the assorted rogues, harridans and reprobates played by most of the cast of *Last of the Summer Wine*. Such (unsurprising) contrary views are largely because one person's feisty grandpa is another's curmudgeonly old codger.

> He [Victor Meldrew] is a very intelligent man, but he's making out to be a bit stupid or a bit senile to make people laugh, which isn't true. You don't suddenly lose your brain overnight when you turn 50. (Sid, Rugby)

Game - On, but not for the Forty-Niners

In quiz shows, participants were disappointed with the paucity of older contestants, although one such show, *Countdown*, was singled out for praise for its apparent policy on inclusivity. The otherwise invisibility of older contestants was particularly irritating for this audience group, since they believe not only that their experience of life and their general knowledge and expertise developed over their lifetimes are being ignored, but that most of the viewers watching such shows are themselves older people, who would probably enjoy seeing more older people being active and clever. Some viewers commented that, even when quiz and game shows do include older contestants, they are often patronised and "humoured" by the host, as if they need special treatment or had special needs, of the "Can you manage those stairs?" variety.

On game shows, viewers felt patronised when there was a special themed "wrinkly" version of mainstream shows such as *Blind Date*, in which older people end up looking like old fools who are either hankering after their lost youth or bemused by the strange protocols of the game show. This portrayal of older age, no matter how unintentional, as not fully functioning or lost in the modern world plays with the same kinds of assumptions which drive ageist humour, where loss of critical and other faculties is a cause of merriment and disrespect. The issue of making "specials" was also raised in the context of holiday shows, in which older holidaymakers are always seen as a separate category of traveller who deserve their own "pensioners' special", instead of an older person simply being an "ordinary" tourist who has likes and dislikes, needs and preferences in the same way as everyone else. The point made repeatedly was that one's age was not necessarily the principal signifier for an individual and was not the barrier to life's riches and enjoyment that some younger people (and programme makers) seem to believe.

Now You See Us, Now You Don't

In some ways, viewers' irritation with the ways in which older people and ageing in general were portrayed on television was matched by their concern over the invisibility of older people more generally across the television landscape. They often felt marginalised from the TV "community" because their lives were rendered invisible by a bias towards content aimed at younger age groups. Whilst this was often a criticism made against game and quiz shows and soaps, it was widely felt that older people did not feature sufficiently across *all* genres.

> Well, they want the bright young image, don't they? ... you're not expected to have brains in some of these shows, as long as you're decorative. (Mildred, Middlesborough)

The Gender Agenda

Viewers, and especially women, in our study noted that the representation of older age had a very clear gender dimension, and other studies support this concern. Nearly thirty years ago, Petersen (1973) identified that women over the age of 65 represented nearly 6% of the US population, but accounted for only 1.21% of the TV character population. When this finding is compared to one which shows that older men represent 4% of the US population, but accounted for 14% of the TV character population, then it is clear that a dissonance between fact and fiction exists. Other studies showed, for example, that the ratio of male to female characters is 3:1 (Levinson 1973), a finding replicated by a number of later studies (see Aronoff, 1974; Gerbner, Gross, Signorielli, & Morgan, 1980; Greenberg, Korzenny, & Atkin, 1980; Signorielli, 1982; Dail, 1988). The work of Gerbner et al. found that, whilst women characters in their early 20s outnumber men of similar age, this falls to four or five times *below* the number of men as they grow older and Aronoff concluded that the average woman character was 10 years younger than the average male character. Signorielli noted that older women characters were less likely to have a job, rarely had an occupation outside the home and were most commonly portrayed as housewives. More recently, Robinson &

Decoding Discrimination

Skill's study found that 68% of TV characters over 50 were men, although they conclude that the percentage of women aged 50-65 years has increased since the gloomier evidence of the 1970s. Vernon, Williams, Phillips, & Wilson (1991) argue that, following their content analysis of 139 programmes and 2,211 characters, older men are more likely to be portrayed positively on 7 out of 9 desirable traits and older women more likely to be depicted negatively on 6 out of 7 undesirable traits.

The broad view from the focus groups was that, while actors generally seem to disappear from television once they turn 50, there are at least some good roles for men, even if older women are a rarity on television. Viewers had a number of ideas about why there were so few older women on the screens, such as: women need to be young and beautiful to be on television; older women are assumed to be off-putting to a young audience, because they are unattractive; and older women have nothing to offer.

> It's about being young, slim and glamorous, isn't it? The blonder you are, the more likely you are to get on. (Cynthia, Brighton)

> Part of it is about history, where it's always men who are the heroes, who go out to work. But that isn't true anymore and yet it still lingers on. There are lots of heroes who are women, but you don't hear about them. (Val, London)

Growing Old Invisibly

When you get documentaries, they are always about men, but there have been lots of women who have done courageous things, good things. Where are those stories? (Sheila, Leamington)

Societal beliefs about attractiveness and youth which, in the case of women, are reflected and perpetuated by the media, contribute (Vasil & Wass, 1993) to their under-representation in what has been referred to elsewhere as the "sexist double standard of ageing" (England, Kuhn & Gardner, 1981), which renders older women virtually invisible across many media. In our study, the three areas where older women were regarded by the viewers as having a more positive presence on television were as: news presenters, e.g. Julia Somerville, Anna Ford; as matriarchs in soaps and dramas, e.g. Pauline Fowler , the character in the BBC soap *EastEnders*; or as wise-ass crones, e.g. *The Golden Girls*.

Daytime TV – a Panacea for the "Olds"?

A number of viewers were annoyed that so many chat shows and other forms of "talk TV" seem preoccupied with sex, sleaze, tragedy and perversion and that the shows' complete lack of interest in the experiences of "real" and "ordinary" people in general, let alone older people in particular, indicated both the lack of interest that programme makers have with the lives of real people, but also their distance from an understanding of what viewers want to see. To some extent, this is reflected in the low levels of reported viewing for morning and afternoon programmes, because older audiences feel alienated from much of the content of such shows. Burnett (1991) and Huston et al. (1992) both suggest that older audiences prefer information (e.g. news, documentaries and public affairs) over entertainment. However, a study of older age and broadcasting conducted for Age Concern England and the Independent Television Commission (Hanley, 2000) suggests that the success of quiz shows in afternoon time-slots is because viewers absolve themselves from suggestions of time-wasting when watching daytime TV by preferring factual programmes or games of intellectual skill.

Whilst there was much enthusiasm for lifestyle programming, such as gardening, DIY/makeovers and cookery programmes, viewers in our study tended to prefer those programmes because they were relaxing to watch (entertainment), rather than providing "genuine" information or education. This was because many felt that the programmes concentrated more on the aesthetic of the content, the background, the landscape, and the personality of the presenter(s), and less on providing, say, a recipe which could be written down and followed. Moreover, these shows were again regarded as being geared towards younger people, with their focus on "instant" transformation. Whilst viewers appreciated the nice decor and the witty chefs, many having a particular fondness for the Two Fat Ladies and Keith Floyd, they nonetheless wondered why proper recipes could not make a comeback. Viewers were keen to say that they did not want a boring succession of pot roasts and casseroles (they know how to cook those dishes anyway); rather, they would like to see a mix of interesting ideas, but also practical hints and tips, especially for those people on a budget, who would obviously include low-income families as well as the many older people who are dependent on the State pension.

Growing Old Invisibly

Speaking Ill of the Old

As well as the largely negative images of older age on television, the participants in our study were also concerned about the casual and routine way in which older people are described as "pensioners" or "the elderly" or "confused" or "frail". In the same way that people with any kind of mental health problem object to being routinely described as "schizo" (see Glasgow University Media Group, 1995), so older people are often given the label of suffering from "dementia" when they might have any one of a number of problems, which may or may not be age-related. Viewers were irritated by the way in which all older people are bracketed together as one homogenous mass of old age pensioners (OAPs), with no attempt by programme makers to differentiate people, even on crude bases such as gender, (dis)ability or employment status.

> We're up against the general discrimination that women face every day of their lives and all we're seeing on television is that reflection.. The people [in the media industry] who make these decisions, they're carrying around these incorrect ideas about society as well. (Anne, Coventry)

Older women were often scathing about the way in which the news media would try and undermine the desirability or sexual potency of older women by, say, using "then" and "now" photographs, or suggesting that Barbara Windsor, for example, looked "good for her age". There were a number of comments about the news media's preoccupation with allocating older people to the "victim" role and escalating a climate of fear, completely ignoring the fact that older people are far less likely to be victims of crime than young men.

Why We Get the Television We (Do Not) Deserve

When asked why we get what we get on TV, older viewers are in little doubt about the reasons. Almost unanimously, they agreed that this was because most people who work in TV are young and therefore work out of a young person's sense, sensibility and experience.

> ....it seems to me that they [the programme makers] are still targeting young people and not taking into consideration the views of older people. (Beth, Bolton)

> I think the advertisers are trying to get at young people with disposable incomes. (Robin, Watford)

There was a strong view, for example, that young writers cannot write convincing parts for older characters – and that the solution to this is either for young writers to do better homework or for commissioning editors to employ older writers.

> I think mainly the ones that write for TV, well, they're not much older than the audiences they're targeting, so they've got the same mentality. (Brian, Wolverhampton)

Participants also engaged in discussions which centred on whether or not TV merely reflected the ageist values of the broader community. After all, it might not be entirely fair to blame TV for merely putting up a mirror to the face of the "community" to see how it thinks about older people. However, viewers suggested that the broadly negative and disrespectful ways in which older people are portrayed on TV has a direct relationship to the way they are treated in their real lives.

> Older people don't have the respect of society. You're shoved off the edge as soon as you're over fifty or even younger, so why should television reflect anything else?' (Kate, Bolton)

There was also a view that the ways in which older people are treated by young people in children's programmes, but also in other genres, provides the "wrong" kinds of cues and role behaviours, so that young people come to believe that disrespecting older people is OK and even ordinary.

> All these programmes, like the soaps, *Home and Away* - the parents are always being put down by their children and that gets me, because not all families are like that. It gives the wrong message.
> (Brian, Wolverhampton)

Cause for Applause – a Few Good Ones

Notwithstanding the range of criticisms described above, which were as much about absences as presences, there were a number of programmes and programme types which found considerable favour amongst our viewers. These characters and/or shows did not necessarily always

Decoding Discrimination

portray older people in a positive light, but they tended to draw more fully rounded characters, of people as ordinary, displaying the usual range of positive, neutral and negative behaviours. Quite often, it was precisely the ordinariness of an older person going about her or his day-to-day lives which viewers found most pleasing, because it is precisely that ordinariness with which they themselves can identify. Individual characters that were often mentioned include battling women, such as Peggy Mitchell, Dot Cotton and Pauline Fowler *(EastEnders),* as well as DCI Morse *(Inspector Morse)* and Martin Crane *(Frasier).* Whilst there were often mixed views about whether some characters were contributing the "right" kind of image, what viewers liked about them was that they were individuals with a life and a personality first and then, occasionally, they were involved in a storyline which figured age specifically. Characters and shows which portrayed older people absolutely *not* acting their age, being challenging, funny and/or rebellious (or even sexy) such as *Steptoe and Son, Waiting for God, Open All Hours, Rising Damp* and *Last of the Summer Wine* were especially liked for these reasons.

> In *Coronation Street,* those characters are quite strong, the older ones. You think of Rita. I know they make fun of her hair, which gets bigger and bigger, but she's a very positive woman who hasn't taken a back seat, but who carries on working and has developed. Her shop is changing into a post office, so I find her really positive.
>
> (Wendy, Hartlepool)

Growing Old Invisibly

People like Trevor Macdonald - the way he presents the news, the dignity, and he speaks so fluently. You can understand the language he uses; it isn't full of big words. (Jim, Rugby)

Older presenters like Michael Parkinson know how to handle people, to draw them out, to be funny, and can adapt to new situations. These new ones have made their money out of being a pop star or something and haven't got those skills and it is very, very noticeable. (Bill, Watford)

Although lifestyle programmes were often criticised for their "youth" orientation, viewers nonetheless appreciated them because they often showed older people being expert, showing their skills and providing a positive face (quite literally) to age and experience. This was particularly the case with TV cooks such as Keith Floyd, the Two Fat Ladies and even Fanny Craddock, the doyenne of dinner party cooking from the 1960s, all of whom were identified as making a positive contribution to improving the portrayal of older people. Programmes like *Antiques Roadshow* were also enjoyed as much for the display of wisdom and expertise on the part of the older presenters/experts as for the content. This programme was often commented upon as one that many people in our study liked watching, not least because many of the artefacts discussed were objects which people remembered from their own past (or present) or could otherwise identify with. In a fairly significant way, at least for these audiences, the programme celebrates a halcyon past, which is imbued with a sense of solid and sturdy values, "proper" craftsmanship and a regard for the importance of time and place; this might seem gloriously old-fashioned to modern sensibilities, yet it makes real sense and appears to provide real enjoyment to older viewers.

Thinking Allowed

While the older people who took part in the study were, on the whole, pleased to be given the opportunity to express their views about television, they were sceptical that broadcasters would actually *do* anything concrete as a result of their reactions and suggestions. However, if broadcasters are serious in their commitment to represent the full plurality of the audience and to respond to the viewing needs of all their diverse constituents, then the voice of the "grey viewer" must be attended to and acted upon. One of the most significant issues to arise from this study was the question of balance, of older people as characters in mainstream popular programming or as presenters of and participants in fact-based programmes. Crucially, the ways in which older people feature in the television landscape is extremely problematic, not simply in terms of where they *are,* but where they are *not*. If, as Kellner (1990) suggests, television stands at the centre of our symbolic universe, then both the nature of the symbols and the nature of the world must be changed if the hegemonic orthodoxies currently peddled are to be ruptured by the realities of real people's real lives. And part of our own concern, as well as that of many of those older people who worked with us, is about who has control over televisual images and in whose likenesses are those images constructed.

We argue that there is a strong relationship between the body of published research on the portrayal of older people and the way older people themselves perceive that portrayal. This is significant in that much of the published work dates from the 1970s and was conducted on US audiences watching US programmes. From our study, it is clear that older people in the UK today have analysed TV output in Britain and come to broadly the same conclusions. Older TV consumers are an informed and knowing audience: they recognise the patterns of employment in the industry and they understand the role of advertisers and their desire to target generational groups whom they perceive to have high levels of disposable income. Part of the problem is, arguably, that the people who work in the industry and who write, edit, direct and commission programmes are mostly *not* older people; therefore, they necessarily have to *imagine* what an older person might be like or how they would act. This is not to argue, though, that a younger writer is incapable of constructing a credible older character; rather it is to suggest that such constructions will necessarily be informed by a perspective and an experiential standpoint which is intrinsically different to that of someone who *is* older. It is not necessarily worse, but it *is* palpably different. As members of the licence-paying public, older viewers have as much right to be heard as anyone else and can reasonably expect to see images and representations of themselves, in all their infinite diversity, across the spectrum of television programming. If television is a public space for us, the viewers, then strategies must surely be found to challenge and to change those public spaces, so that they become a bit more representative and accessible for television's many publics.

Postscript

One City Council has been consulting with local (older) people to find out what they want to see happening in the city to make life better for them. One consultee said she wanted to see more police officers on the beat. She said that the only place that she ever saw a police officer was on television. There are clearly more police officers on TV, pro rata, than there are in the population, although there has never been a study to demonstrate this fact. But if we accept Hacker's (1951) suggestion that fictional portrayals are an indication of a groups' social status - and if this still holds true half a century later - we obviously think less of our older people than we do of our police officers, which seems to be another odd contradiction.

References

Ansello, E. F. (1978, November). *Broadcast images: The elderly woman on television.* Paper presented at the Annual Scientific Meeting of the Gerontological Society, Dallas, TX.

Aronoff, C. (1974). Old age in prime time. *Journal of Communication, 24* (4), 86-87.

Bourne, S. (1998*). Black in the British frame: Black people in British film and television, 1896-1996.* London: Cassell.

Broadcasting Standards Council. (1994). *Perspectives of women in television.* London: Author.

Broadcasting Standards Council. (1995). *Perspectives of disability in broadcasting.* London: Author.

Burnett, J. J. (1991). Examining the media habits of the affluent elderly. *Journal of Advertising Research, 31* (5), 33-41.

Communications Research Group. (1999). *Too old for TV?: The portrayal of older people on television.* London: Age Concern England.

Cumberbatch, G., & Negrine, R. (1992). *Images of disability on television.* London: Routledge.

Dail, P. (1988). Prime-time television portrayals of older adults in the context of family life. *Gerontologist, 28* (5), 700-706.

Davis, R. H., & Davis, J. A. (1985). *TV's image of the elderly: A practical guide for change.* Lexington, MA: Lexington Books.

England, P., Kuhn A., & Gardner, T. (1981). The ages of men and women in magazine advertisements. *Journalism Quarterly, 58,* 468-471.

Gerbner, G., Gross, L., Signorielli, N., & Morgan, M. (1980). Ageing with television: Images on television dramas and conceptions of social reality. *Journal of Communication, 30,* 37-47.

Glasgow University Media Group. (1995). *Mass media representations of mental health/illness.* Glasgow: Author.

Greenberg, B. S., Korzenny, F., & Atkin, C. K. (1980). Trends in the portrayal of the elderly. In B. S. Greenberg (Ed.), *Life of television: Content analyses of U.S. TV drama* (pp. 23-33). Norwood, NJ: Ablex.

Hacker, H. (1951). Women as a minority group. *Social Forces, 30,* 39-44.

Hanley, P. (2000). *Age in the frame: Television and the over 50s: a study of portrayal, representation and viewing.* London: Age Concern England.

Harris, A., & Feinberg, J. (1977). Television and ageing: Is what you see what you get? *Gerontologist, 17* (5), 464-468.

Healey, T., & Ross, K. (2002). Growing old invisibly: Older viewers talk television. *Media, Culture & Society,* 24 (1), 105-120.

Huston, A. C., Donnerstein, E., Fairchild, H., Fesbach, N. D., Katz, P. A., Murray, J. P., et al. (1992). *Big world, small screen: The role of television in American society.* Lincoln: University of Nebraska.

Kellner, D. (1990). Advertising and consumer culture. In J. Downing, A. Mohammadi & A. Sreberny-Mohammadi (Eds.), *Questioning the media: A critical introduction* (pp. 242-254). Newbury Park, CA: Sage.

Kent, R. (Ed.) (1994). *Measuring media audiences*. London: Routledge.

Labour Market Trends (1995-). London: Central Statistical Office.

Levinson, R. (1973). From Olive Oyle to Sweet Polly Purebread: Sex role stereotypes and televised cartoons. *Journal of Popular Culture, 9,* 561-572.

Northcote, H. C. (1975). Too young, too old: Age in the world of television. *Gerontologist, 15* (2), 184-186.

Petersen, M. (1973). The visibility and image of old people on television. *Journalism Quarterly, 50,* 569-573.

Robinson, J. D., & Skill, T. (1995). The invisible generation: Portrayals of the elderly on prime-time television. *Communication Report, 8,* 111-119.

Ross, K. (1997). But where's me in it?: Disability, broadcasting and the audience. *Media, Culture & Society, 19,* 669-677.

Signorielli, N. (1982). Marital status in television drama: a case of reduced options. *Journal of Broadcasting, 26* (2), 585-597.

Vasil, L., & Wass, H. (1993). Portrayal of the elderly in the media: a literature review and implications for educational gerontologists. *Educational Gerontology, 19,* 71-85.

Vernon, J. A., Williams, J. A., Jr., Phillips, T., & Wilson, J. (1991). Media stereotyping: A comparison of the way elderly women and men are portrayed on prime-time television. *Journal of Women & Ageing, 2* (4), 55-68.

3

IS THE WORLD MOVING? CHANGING WOMEN, UNCHANGED MEN IN POST-INDUSTRIAL BRITAIN[1]

Sara Delamont

The title of this chapter comes from George Gissing's novel *The odd women* (1893/1980), in which a feminist tells her friend that "The world is moving!" (p. 336). I used that novel as one benchmark for my book *Changing women, unchanged men?* (2001). I wanted to set the data on gender in Britain in the 1990s against some fixed earlier point. Change has to be measured over some definite period and I thought that, in the absence of any relevant sociology from the 1890s, a realist novel about gender would have to do. *The odd women* is not a famous novel, but it deals with nineteenth century feminism, especially the feminism of educated upper middle class ladies in London. Its heroines are working to ensure that ladies who cannot, or do not, marry are trained so that they are able to earn a respectable living. The book offers several negative possibilities: loveless marriages; shop work; prostitution; alcoholism; trying to run a school; being a governess or a companion. These are all seen as degrading and financially precarious. Marriage with love is fine, but the young woman who marries without love to escape shop work comes to a tragic end. The two heroines, who have chosen to be celibate spinsters, are seen as pioneers of a

---

[1] I am grateful to Rosemary Bartle Jones, who word-processed this paper.

new way of life: a respectable alternative to marriage. However, in 1893 they are revolutionary and their views and behaviour are evidence of the dangerous radical ideas held by "New Women".

In the 1990s, commentaries by many media pundits, and by a few social scientists, were proposing that once again there were socially dangerous feminists around, especially in London, undermining marriage, society and men. The commentators in the media included both men and women. Melanie Phillips was perhaps the most vehement, with a litany of complaints about unspecified feminists who had undermined society (see, for example, Phillips, 1999): this paralleled her earlier complaints about education (Phillips, 1996). Amongst the social scientists were Geoffrey Dench (1994; 1995) and Norman Dennis (1997; see also Dennis and Erdos, 1992; 2000). Both had done excellent studies of contemporary Britain thirty years before: Dench on the Maltese in London (1975) and Dennis, with Henriques and Slaughter, on Yorkshire miners (1956). In the 1990s though, they had become paranoid about feminists, again unspecified and uncited, who were unmanning British men and destroying British society. In the USA, Fukuyama (1999) took a similar line.

In the sphere of more sober commentaries upon research results - as opposed to feverish polemics based on little or no data - there was a slightly different, although related, argument. In a book aimed at the general public, Harriet Harman (1993) argued for a proposition called "Twenty first century women, twentieth century man?" Research undertaken in the USA by Lois Weis (1990) and in the UK by Janet Holland and her collaborators (1993, 1998) both found that young women were adapting better to a post-industrial society than young men. Lois Weis studied young people in Rochester, a city in New York State, which was a prosperous industrial centre in the nineteenth century, but has fallen into post-industrial recession in the last thirty years. Young women recognised that the old job market, and with it the old division of labour, had gone for ever and had plans to get credentials to attend the university and leave Rochester. The young men had, in contrast, unrealistic hopes of traditional male industrial jobs in Rochester, which would enable them to support wives who ran traditional homes. The Women Risk and Aids Project (WRAP) and the Men Risks and Aids Project (MRAP) in England produced a parallel set of findings about sexuality and intimate behaviour (Holland, Ramazanoglu & Sharpe, 1993; Holland, Ramazanoglu, Sharpe & Thomson, 1998).

Against this background, I set out to write a book on gender in Britain. I had written one twenty years before (Delamont, 1980b), when feminist sociology was just getting up steam, but when the public and social science "discourse of derision" against feminism and feminist sociology was much more muted. The approach of a millennium had, in the 1990s, produced fin de siècle anxieties about gender and sexualities, just as it had in the 1790s and the 1890s. As Elaine Showalter (1997) argues, the trial of Oscar Wilde and the Maud Allen vs. Noel Pemberton-Billing libel case were, for the end of the nineteenth century, symptoms of fin de siècle anxieties about male and female same sex desire. These are classic moral panics, paralleling the fears about New Women.

As I wrote the book, there were three intellectual debates swirling about which had to be treated seriously in any work of sociology: firstly, was Britain in a postmodern era or only a post-industrial one?; secondly, was a postmodern theoretical perspective the only one worth discussing or was it a sinister French diversion from serious social science?; thirdly, did the new perspective of evolutionary psychology render sociology itself irrelevant?

Each debate is explained briefly, starting with evolutionary psychology's challenge.

Evolutionary Psychology

Evolutionary psychology is the latest in a 150-year-long series of outbursts of popular science publicised whenever women achieve, or even campaign for, any social change in Britain. Feminists are routinely attacked with ideas that anti-feminists claim are the latest scientific truth. In the 1840-1870 era, when first wave feminists campaigned for academic secondary education, higher education, and the opening up of the medical profession, there was a popular scientific theory that intelligence and intellectual capacity were directly related to head and brain size. Men had bigger heads than women and only males had a skull capacity to learn Latin and Greek, attend university, or study medicine. This popular scientific theory was overthrown when the skull measurements of Australian aboriginals became known. Aboriginal women had bigger heads, and therefore more cranial capacity, than middle-class White men in Britain; so the gross capacity of the brain could no longer serve as a "scientific" reason to prevent young women learning algebra or physics.

In the last thirty years of the nineteenth century, the continuing campaigns for education and respectable work, plus the right to vote, to sit on juries and local authorities and become lawyers and accountants, were greeted with a new "scientific" theory: energy conservation and social Darwinism. A theory spread that the human body had limited resources and, if they were spent on brain work (learning Greek verbs), menstruation would cease and infertility rise. As the White middle classes sent their daughters to school, they would be outbred by the lower orders. In the USA, the fear was that new Catholic immigrants from Ireland, Italy and Poland would outbreed the Protestants; in the UK, social class was the central concern. The theory was particularly associated with G. Stanley Hall (1904), author of a 1200 page two-volume work on *Adolescence*. For these writers, Darwin's ideas of evolution as a contest between species in the natural world could be used in the social world to explain the struggle between classes or races. A class or race would only survive if it bred strong children and so the White middle classes must not be "outbred" by other classes and races.

After the First World War, feminism in the UK and the USA lost much of its intellectual clout under the impact of Freudianism. Because of the powerful impact the English translations of Freud's ideas had had in helping the mental casualties of the Great War, because they were new, revolutionary, deeply shocking to the older generation, and because they rendered first wave feminism's ideas about morality, sex, gender, sexuality and celibacy obsolete, Freudianism destroyed the credibility of that feminism. The new, second wave, social feminism of the years 1920-1968, with its emphasis on issues relevant to married women, such as welfare provision, birth control, child health, maternity care and family allowances, was a post-Freudian feminism. The 1939-1945 War saw some social change for women, especially in education (women students admitted to the famous London teaching hospitals, for example) and employment. As soon as it ended, as Wilson (1980) shows, a new variety of Freudianism, Bowlby's theory of maternal deprivation (see Rutter, 1972) became the popular scientific fashion. A popular ideology, based in science, that all babies needed full-time mothers, was a wonderful impetus to get women out of the labour market, to free jobs for returning servicemen.

Decoding Discrimination

Since the beginnings of third wave, or contemporary, feminism in the 1960s, there have been six popular scientific "theories" advanced, which have all been used to argue that third wave feminism is flying in the face of "science" and is therefore doomed to fail; but is, in the mean time, damaging British society and making "real women" desperately unhappy. In the 1960s, there were claims that hormones made women unstable and that many desirable qualities, including spatial reasoning, were carried on the Y chromosome. It was also argued that violence was due to testosterone and/or the Y chromosome; so, as well as giving males advantages as airline pilots and architects, it did mean that they were more likely to become axe murderers and street fighters. (Throughout my time as a PhD student, the head of my department, a Freudian, told me that I was only doing a doctorate because I suffered from penis envy, for which I should have therapy; and my flatmate's boyfriend, a psychology lecturer, told me that women could not do research because they did not have a Y chromosome).

In the 1970s, there was a vogue for sociobiology, which used arguments from animal behaviour to state that male and female physiology precluded men from nurturing and women from having careers. In the 1980s, a new theory of hemispheres came along, which stated that, in Western societies and races, males have an impermeable membrane between the left and right hemispheres of the brain, so that the left (emotional, intuitive) side is entirely separate from the right (rational, dispassionate, "scientific") side. In Western women and all "orientals", such as Japanese, the membrane is permeable, so these brains cannot "do" rational objective science without emotions swilling into the right side (Moir & Jessel, 1989).

In the 1990s, the latest of these popular scientific theories was evolutionary psychology. This is essentially sociobiology back again, with a sexier and more authoritative name. Basically, the argument is that the behaviour patterns that allowed homo erectus or early homo sapiens to survive ice ages and interpluvials 50,000 or 100,000 years ago are now hard-wired into the species, so that it is not *possible* for men or women to change. Therefore, anyone who tries to encourage men to do more child care or women to do more physics or financial management is flying in the face of 100,000 years of evolution. The fact that we know, and can know, nothing about human behaviour among early sapiens 50,000 years ago, and cannot extrapolate evidence from primates (baboons, chimpanzees or gorillas) or the few hunting and gathering races left (!kung bushmen, Ituri pygmies) seems not to bother these authors. It is equally absurd to ignore the plasticity of sapiens as a species: humans have rapidly changed behaviour over the past 10,000 years, compared, for example, with pandas and gorillas. The behaviours which allowed the Inuit to live in Alaska, the Maoris to live in New Zealand and the Pathan to live in Pakistan, and for descendants one generation away from these cultures all to drive taxis in New York together, are hardly immutable. Overall, I decided that evolutionary psychology was merely the latest in a long line of pseudo-scientific popularisations designed to derail feminism, and I could briefly dismiss it and write a sociological book. Postmodernism was more of a problem.

Postmodern Theory

The rise of postmodern theory in literature, cultural studies and sociology is more serious than the latest popular scientific fad. There is an excellent introduction to postmodernist ideas in Lyon (1999) and neither space nor a necessity to rehearse them here. The challenges posed to feminist ideas are, however, serious, and need summarising (Barrett & Phillips, 1992). Liberal feminism, which is a central part of feminist sociology, deploys sound data on sex inequalities to argue for improvements made by rational, fair-minded people. Postmodernism challenges the foundations of "sound data", because it rejects the very idea of objectivity, which underpins "sound data". Marxist or socialist feminism, which has been important in feminist sociology, especially in theory and analyses of work and domestic life, is equally undermined by postmodernism's intellectual destruction of "class" as an analytic category. Radical or separatist feminism (Walby, 1990), perhaps the least influential element in feminist sociology, except in work on sexualities and lesbianism, is undermined by postmodernism's rejection of the categories of sex and gender. So, too, with Black feminism, because of postmodernism's rejection of "race". Feminists and feminist sociologists have fought back: for example, Brodribb (1992), Walby (1992), Hoff (1994) and Bell & Klein (1996).

However, just as many feminists have seized on postmodernism as a potential "ism" that shares feminism's doubts about objectivity, the Enlightenment Project and the canonisation of dead White men: for example, Butler (1900; 1999), Lather (1991; 2001). Sandra Harding, the feminist philosopher of science, is one such convert (see Harding, 2000).

My own attitude is deeply ambivalent and draws on a historical parallel. In the years after 1918, the intellectual coherence of first wave feminism was destroyed by Freudianism. The new, difficult, but revolutionary continental idea swept through intellectual circles (male and female) and destroyed the epistemology of feminism. It took forty to fifty years to organise a new epistemology for third wave feminism. (Second wave was an essentially

Is the World Moving?

practical, reformist movement, not an intellectual one). Postmodernism is the Freudianism of the early twenty-first century. It has the *potential* to destroy the epistemological foundations of contemporary feminism. It also makes it much harder to write a straightforward "factual" book, such as *Sex roles and the school* (Delamont, 1980a, 1990) or *The sociology of women* (Delamont, 1980b). Both the state of sociology and the state of feminism are very different from what they were in those halcyon days. So too, of course, is the UK, and that is the subject of the third intellectual debate.

A Postmodern Society or a Post-Industrial Society?

Alongside the rise of postmodernism as a theory, there is a parallel claim that some capitalist countries have passed from being industrial societies to post-industrial ones, and thence become postmodern, or entered a state of reflexive modernity. This proposition, put forward by Lash, Urry, Giddens and Beck in the early 1990s (see Beck, Giddens & Lash, 1994) is addressed in Lash and Urry's evocatively titled *Economies of signs and space* (1994). According to these theories, men and women have become citizens of a new type of society, unless they are marooned in an underclass. The unsophisticated commentators discussed earlier (Dench and Dennis, furiously defending a traditional division of labour, undermined, as they see it, by chattering-class Islington feminists; Harman, bemoaning the failure of men to adapt to the twenty-first century) are, although they do not explicitly address the point, in dispute with Lash, Urry, Giddens and Beck. Dench and Dennis are the social science equivalents of the young men Weis found in Rochester, yearning for metal-bashing jobs for men that pay wages which are high enough to support wives who are not in paid employment, but who run the home. Harman is, in effect, claiming that men have not adjusted their heads to the emotional and practical demands of life in an era of reflexive modernity or an economy of signs and space.

This is not a straightforward context in which to write a book. Matters are complicated by the explosion of research on women, on gender and on men and masculinity, and the concomitant expansion of the sociological gaze into new vistas. Since Ann Oakley began her PhD thesis on housework (see 1974a, 1974b), feminist sociologists (men and women) have pioneered the doubling in size of the academic field of sociology. There has been the unfolding of eight topics within what was previously the "private" sphere and the examination of new issues in the old areas of sociology, such as work. The sociology of politics and religion may have declined in importance, but in the other big areas, education, work, inequality, class, health and science, the research landscape has been transformed by the crossing over of the feminist agenda.

In the "private" sphere, the eight new topics are: housework, food and drink, caring, leisure, money, violence, intimacy and emotions, and sexualities. In the "public" sphere, issues of sexualities, intimacy and emotions, along with violence and harassment, have provided novel research perspectives on education, work, health and science. The sociology of class, social mobility and class identity has been transformed by the feminist-inspired focus on women as class members and class actors. In addition, there is the wholesale development of a vibrant research area: masculinities and the new men's studies, closely allied and overlapping with the now established and growing field of queer theory (Mac an Ghaill, 1996). This explosion in new sociological topics and the growth in empirical research which treats gender

Is the World Moving?

seriously mean that any new book in this area has to be either absurdly long or ruthlessly selective.

The Central Question

The central question addressed, therefore, is: have women changed, while men have failed to do so? To explore this, we need to know whether or not women have changed (against some fixed time schedule) and whether or not men have changed over the same period. Change in this context has to mean in relation to both attitudes and behaviour. I took the time-frames to be a half-century and a century: that is, I looked at men and women in Britain in 1893, 1951 and 2001. If those arguing that the UK has become a postmodern economy are correct, then the old employment-based identities of work, class, locality, sex and marital status should be in rapid retreat, being replaced by multiple identities, each rooted in consumption rather than production. To take an example: when Dennis, Henriques & Slaughter (1956) studied Ashton, the Yorkshire mining town, in the 1950s, it had been there for fifty years. Men were miners; their identity was grounded in that work; they were working class, Ashtoners, Yorkshire men, union members, straight, family men, husbands, sons and fathers. The women were miners' wives, mothers and daughters and were also working class, Ashtoners, Yorkshire women. The production system provided the identities. Similar arguments could be advanced for the Hull fishermen and their wives (Tunstall, 1972); the London dockers and their wives (Hill, 1976); and even the Luton car workers (Goldthorpe & Lockwood, 1968).

Clearly, all those industries have gone from those places: no mines in Ashton, fishing in Hull, dockwork in London or car plants in Luton survive in 2001. Gone, too, are the "communities" centred on those industries as they existed in 1901 or 1951. However, it is less clear that employment and class *identities* have gone for men or women, to be replaced by multiple selves. There is an argument that men and women *always had multiple selves*: among miners, it was possible to be actively religious or not, to prefer whippets to soccer or bowls to cricket, to prefer gardening to the pub or the brass band practice to the union meeting. It is possible that, if researchers had gone out to search for multiple identities in Ashton in 1893, 1901 or 1951, they would have found them among the men. However, researchers in 1951 did not frame their research questions around a search for multiple selves. The data on the women in Ashton in Dennis, Henriques & Slaughter (1956) are limited and reported in a stereotyped way, as Frankenberg (1976) pointed out long ago. It is equally possible that women in Ashton had multiple identities in 1893, 1901 and 1951, but no one looked for them.

Atkinson & Housley (2003) demonstrate that much of the emphasis in current postmodern theorising on multiple selves and identities was central to the ideas of G. H. Mead a century ago in Chicago. If Mead argued for the existence of multiple selves in the 1890s (see Mead, 1934), they cannot be the product of any post-industrial society. There is no doubt that some identities have changed. In 1893, British men and women were exhorted to have an identity as citizens of a global empire and that empire still existed in 1951. No one in contemporary Britain has that identity any more and the idea of a commonwealth identity is not powerful. The Commonwealth Institute has abandoned its educational mission and it seems unlikely that either men or women ground their sense of self in the idea of "commonwealth". There have been shifts in the extent to which identity is grounded in being *British*, as opposed to being English, Scottish, Welsh, Irish, or Ulster Protestant.

Is the World Moving?

Mac an Ghaill (1994) found that white English teenage boys *felt* that they lacked an identity that African-Caribbean, Irish, or Muslim English boys had. No such feelings were reported from young women. The devolution agenda has certainly *reinforced* Scottish and Welsh identities in those nations, and it is hard to claim these are about consumption rather than class or work or that they are based in postmodernity or a post-industrial economy.

The Solutions and the Outcome

In the end, I wrote the book in ten chapters. Apart from the introduction and conclusion, there is a theory chapter that debates postmodernism, three chapters on childhood, adolescence and young adults and four chapters on adulthood. These deal with: stigma, deviance and the body; consumption and locality; work; and domestic life. Each reviews evidence and then examines whether or not men or women have changed since 1893 or 1951. In the majority of cases, the evidence shows that class differences are more divisive in Britain than those of gender and that, because of class divisions, lives of males and females are not fundamentally different from those of their grandparents in 1951 or their great-, great-, great-, great-grandparents in 1893. It will be interesting to see what has changed by 2051.

References

Atkinson, P., & Housley, W. (2003). *Interactionism: An essay in social amnesia.* London: Sage.

Barrett, M., & Phillips, A. (Eds.) (1992). *Destabilizing theory: Contemporary feminist debates.* Cambridge: Polity Press.

Beck, U., Giddens, A., & Lash, S. (1994). *Reflexive modernization: Politics, tradition and aesthetics in the modern social order.* Cambridge: Polity Press.

Bell, D., & Klein, R. (Eds.) (1996). *Radically speaking: Feminism reclaimed.* London: Zed Books.

Brodribb, S. (1992). *Nothing mat(t)ers: A feminist critique of postmodernism.* North Melbourne, Victoria: Spinifex Press.

Butler, J. (1990). *Gender trouble: Feminism and the subversion of identity.* New York: Routledge.

Butler, J. (1999). *Gender trouble: Feminism and the subversion of identity.* (2nd ed.) New York: Routledge.

Delamont, S. (1980a). *Sex roles and the school.* London: Methuen.

Delamont, S. (1980b). *The sociology of women: An introduction.* London: George Allen & Unwin.

Delamont, S. (1990). *Sex roles and the school.* (2nd ed.) London: Routledge.

Delamont, S. (2001). *Changing women, unchanged men?: Sociological perspectives on gender in a post-industrial society.* Buckingham: Open University Press.

Dench, G. (1975). *Maltese in London: A case-study in the erosion of ethnic consciousness.* London: Routledge & Kegan Paul.

Dench, G. (1994). *The frog, the prince & the problem of men.* London: Neanderthal Books.

Dench, G. (1995). *Transforming men: Changing patterns of dependency and dominance in gender relations.* New Brunswick, NJ: Transaction Publishers.

Dennis, N. (1997). *The invention of permanent poverty.* London: IEA Health & Welfare Unit.

Dennis, N., Henriques, F., & Slaughter, C. (1956). *Coal is our life: An analysis of a Yorkshire mining community.* London: Eyre & Spottiswoode.

Dennis, N., & Erdos, G. (1992). *Families without fatherhood.* London: IEA Health & Welfare Unit.

Dennis, N., & Erdos, G. (2000). *Families without fatherhood.* (3rd ed.) London: Institute for the Study of Civil Society.

Frankenberg, R. (1976). "In the production of their lives, men (?) ... ": Sex and gender in British community studies. In D. L. Barker & S. Allen (Eds.), *Sexual divisions and society: Process and change* (pp. 25-51). London: Tavistock Publications.

Fukuyama, F. (1999). *The great disruption: Human nature and the reconstitution of social order.* London: Profile Books.

Gissing, G. (1980). *The odd women.* London: Virago. (Original work published 1893).

Goldthorpe, J. H., Lockwood, D., Bechhofer, F., & Platt, J. (1968). *The affluent worker in the class structure.* Cambridge: Cambridge University Press.

Hall, G. S. (1904). *Adolescence: Its psychology and its relation to physiology, anthropology, sociology, sex, crime, religion and education.* (2 vols.) New York: D. Appleton.

Harding, S. (2000). Comment on Hekman's "Truth and method: Feminist standpoint theory revisited". In C. Allen & J. A. Howard (Eds.), *Provoking feminisms* (pp. 50-58). Chicago: University of Chicago Press.

Harman, H. (1993). *The century gap: 20th century man, 21st century woman: How both sexes can bridge the century gap.* London: Vermillion.

Hill, S. (1976). *The dockers: Class and tradition in London.* London: Heinemann Educational.

Hoff, J. (1994). Gender as a postmodern category of paralysis. *Women's History Review, 3* (2), 149-168.

Holland, J., Ramazanoglu, C., & Sharpe, S. (1993). *Wimp or gladiator: Contradictions in acquiring masculine sexuality.* London: Tufnell Press.

Holland, J., Ramazanoglu, C., Sharpe, S., & Thomson, R. (1998). *The male in the head: Young people, heterosexuality and power.* London: Tufnell Press.

Lash, S., & Urry, J. (1994). *Economies of signs and space.* London: Sage.

Lather, P. (1991). *Getting smart: Feminist research and pedagogy with/in the postmodern.* New York: Routledge.

Lather, P. (2001). Postmodernism, post-structuralism and post (critical) ethnography. In P. Atkinson, A. Coffey, S. Delamont, J. Lofland, & L. Lofland (Eds.), *Handbook of ethnography* (pp. 477-492). London: Sage.

Lyon, D. (1999.) *Postmodernity.* (2nd ed.) Buckingham: Open University Press.

Mac an Ghaill, M. (1994). *The making of men: Masculinities, sexualities and schooling.* Buckingham: Open University Press.

Mac an Ghaill, M. (Ed.) (1996). *Understanding masculinities: Social relations and cultural arenas.* Buckingham: Open University Press.

Mead, G. H. (1934). *Mind, self, & society, from the standpoint of a social behaviourist.* Chicago: University of Chicago Press.

Moir, A., & Jessel, D. (1989). *Brain sex: The real difference between men and women.* London: Michael Joseph.

Oakley, A. (1974a). *Housewife.* London: Allen Lane.

Oakley, A. (1974b). *The sociology of housework.* London: Martin Robertson.

Phillips, M. (1996). *All must have prizes.* London: Little, Brown.

Phillips, M. (1999). *The sex-change society: Feminised Britain and the neutered male.* London: Social Market Foundation.

Rutter, M. (1972). *Maternal deprivation reassessed.* Harmondsworth: Penguin.

Showalter, E. (1997). *Hystories: Hysterical epidemics and modern culture.* New York: Columbia University Press.

Tunstall, J. (1972). *The fishermen.* (3rd ed.) London: MacGibbon & Kee.

Walby, S. (1990). *Theorising patriarchy.* Oxford: Basil Blackwell.

Walby, S. (1992). Post-post-modernism?: Theorizing social complexity. In M. Barrett & A. Phillips (Eds.),

Destabilizing theory: Contemporary feminist debates (pp. 31-52). Cambridge: Polity Press.

Weis, L. (1990). *Working class without work: High school students in a de-industrializing economy.* New York: Routledge.

Wilson, E. (1980). *Only halfway to paradise: Women in postwar Britain, 1945-1968.* London: Tavistock Publications.

4

THE SOCIAL CONSTRUCTION OF STIGMA IN HEALTH CARE SETTINGS

Tom Mason and Elizabeth Mason-Whitehead[1]

Introduction

There is a well recognised relationship between stigma, prejudice and discrimination and the notion of those groups and individuals who are stigmatised becoming socially excluded (Social Exclusion Unit, 1998). As such socially excluded groups and individuals are lost to the binding force of communities, this fragments and weakens society as a whole (Social Exclusion Unit, 1999). Furthermore, there is growing concern that many socially excluded individuals turn to illicit drugs, alcohol and crime in response to their plight and this leads to a further weakening of social ties, and in turn to an increase in victimisation (Social Exclusion Unit, 2000). Stigma itself is a damaging and destructive term, which usually carries a negative semantic, and few would openly admit to being stigmatising in their social interactions. However, from the extent of marginalised groups that are noted in our society, it is clear that there must be many individuals and institutions that contribute to discriminatory practices, either consciously or subconsciously. In this chapter, we are concerned with stigma in health care settings,

---

[1] This chapter reports on research undertaken by Tom Mason and Elizabeth Mason-Whitehead. It was presented as a paper at Chester by Tom Mason.

particularly in relation to the roles that professionals exercise in the stigmatising process, both in terms of its creation and its perpetuation. As we believe that stigma is fundamentally a social construction, albeit with a recognised practical impact, we will analyse stigma in health care settings from the perspective of social constructionism.

Social Constructionism

Social constructionism is a term that is bandied around academic circles with a frequency that belies its fuller understanding. It is a popular closing retort in intellectual "ping-pong" argumentation to state that "it's not real, it's socially constructed" and, if propounded with enough dismissive finesse, this will usually leave other interlocutors flummoxed. However, we ought not to become either too smug regarding this or too disdainful; as Berger & Luckman (1967, p. 13) put it: "the man in the street inhabits a world that is 'real' to him, albeit in different degrees, and he 'knows', with different degrees of confidence, that this world possesses such and such characteristics. The philosopher, of course, will raise questions about the ultimate status of both this 'reality' and this 'knowledge'". Berger & Luckman, as sociologists, claim to be on a rung somewhere between the man in the street and the philosopher and we, as nurses, claim to be on a rung somewhere between the lay person and Berger & Luckman. There are a number of elements to be dealt with in our quest to understand the nature of social constructionism and this is our first task.

Reality

Given that Berger & Luckman have established that both the lay person and the philosopher will have different degrees of understanding as to the status of what constitutes reality, and also that all readers of these words will at least be on the lay rung of understanding, we will briefly outline the perspectives of two philosophers on the nature of reality. René Descartes (1596-1650), often called the father of modern philosophy, was born in the Touraine region of France and, following an education in the scholastic and humanistic traditions, worked mainly in the field of mathematics. Turning to philosophy, Descartes was concerned that what he perceived, in short his reality, could be doubted. He claimed that he had no way of telling that what he perceived was not a dream, an illusion or a hallucination, and might not be reality. He doubted everything and decided to deconstruct the world by hypothesising an all-deceiving evil genius that confused and confounded him at every stage of his thinking. This deconstruction took him back in his thinking until he was at the point at which he could state his "Cogito, ergo sum" proposition (usually translated as "I think, therefore I am"). The deceiving genius pushed him to this first conclusion in rebuilding his concept of the world; that is, if Descartes perceived something, anything at all - a dream, illusion or hallucination - he must therefore exist. From this starting point, he rebuilt his concept of the world up to, and including, the point of being able to prove the existence of God, to his own satisfaction (Descartes, 1637, 1641/1967).

The second philosopher was Plato (427-347 BCE), who was an Athenian Greek aristocrat and devoted follower of

The Social Construction of Stigma

Socrates. In his central work, the *Republic,* Plato sets out how an ideal society, or an approximation to it, might be justly ruled by philosophers acquiring political power. The most potent image in the *Republic* is the analogy of the cave, now fondly known as Plato's cave, in which he asks the reader to imagine a person born in a cave, fixed to the wall, with no knowledge of the existence of the outside of the cave. Each night, our incumbent sees shadows and flickering lights on the opposite wall and this is his only perception of reality. One night, he is taken down from his fixed position on the wall opposite to the shadows and lights and taken out of the cave to be shown a fire at the cave entrance, with people dancing around it, which was producing the silhouettes on the cave wall. Thus, Plato suggests that the cave dweller now has two realities and, having travelled further afield, with new experiences along the way, he acquires multiple realities. Thus, reality may begin with an internal perception of the self, but also includes a perception of the other, which forms the beginning of social perception (Plato, trans. 1977).

Knowledge

Knowledge is knowledge of something, and to know is to suggest that this something is understood in relation to other things in the world. All things in the world share a relation with other things and Foucault (1970) referred to this as "the order of things". However, there are different approaches to knowledge, with "scientific" being merely one. The word "science" is derived from the Latin *scientia*, which, in turn, is derived from *sciens*, the present participle of *scire*, which means "to know". Scientific knowledge has credence over other types of knowledge, but only for some people. Some believe that other modes of knowledge are superior to scientific knowledge. These other modes of knowledge would include the *authoritarian* mode, which refers to those who are socially or politically defined as being eligible to produce knowledge: "These may be oracles in tribal societies, archbishops in theocratic societies, kings in monarchical societies and individuals occupying scientific roles in technocratic societies" (Nachmias & Nachmias, 1981, p. 5). Other examples of this type of knowledge would include the Pope's undisputed religious knowledge for Catholics and, for Russians, the Soviet Academy of Sciences, which decreed that probability was a non-scientific approach to theory building, in an (abortive) attempt to resolve the conflict between the determinism of dialectical materialism and the theory of probability. In the authoritarian mode, there is a close relationship between the knowledge seeker and the knowledge producer, in which the former requires a high level of confidence in the latter's ability to produce knowledge. Although this type of knowledge can be refuted, it requires a large number of refutations before it is replaced by another type of authority (Nachmias & Nachmias, 1981).

A second type of knowledge is the *mystical* mode, in which people importune knowledge from prophets, divines, gods, mediums and other varied supernatural powers. In one sense, this type of knowledge is similar to the authoritarian mode, but differs as it depends on the manifestation of supernatural indicators, as well as on the psychophysical state of the believer. The production of knowledge in this mode is usually accompanied by rituals and ceremonies, and confidence decreases as the number of disconfirmations increases. The third type of knowledge is the *rationalistic* mode, which involves the belief that all knowledge can be obtained through adherence to forms and rules of logic: "The underlying assumptions of rationalism are that (1) the human mind can apprehend the world independently of observable phenomena and (2) that forms of knowledge exist that are prior to our experiences" (Nachmias & Nachmias, 1981, p. 5). So, the answer to the Zen question: "If a tree falls in a forest and there is no one there to hear it, does it make a sound?" is, for the rationalist: "Yes, it does". In short, the rationalist mode is concerned with what must be true in principle and what is logically possible and permissible.

Reality of Everyday Life

Two founding fathers of sociology gave us an early indication of how to proceed in the quest to understand the reality of everyday life. Durkheim informs us that: "The first and most fundamental rule is to consider social facts as things" (1895/1938, p. 14) and Weber argues that: "Both for sociology in the present sense, and for history, the object of cognition is the subjective meaning-complex of action" (1921/1947, p. 101). These two statements first appear to be contradictory, as the former refers to facts and things as objective elements and the latter indicates the subjective interpretation of human behaviour. However, it is a fact that society does have this dual character "in terms of objective facticity *and* subjective meaning that makes its 'reality *sui generis*'" (Berger & Luckman, 1967, p. 30). Thus, in the creation of stigma, the interesting question is: How does the subjective interpretation of the stigmata, i.e. the Jew, the Black, the Catholic, the gypsy or the disabled, become objective facticities, i.e. greedy, lazy, subversive, sub-human or blameworthy, so that they are perceived as inferior? We will begin to address this question with a brief look at three elements: (a) the here and now; (b) the concept of "I"; and (c) the zones of relevance.

In terms of multiple realities, we can note that there is one that is considered to be the paramount reality: that is, the reality of everyday life. Being conscious creates an awareness that is at its most focused in everyday life. Everyday life imposes itself on our conscious mind in an imperative manner, as we must deal with it in the here and now. In being awake, we apprehend ourselves as being in a constant now, a moment of consciousness that is ever-changing into the next now, and each future now lines up to pass into our instance of awareness to become the past. Consciousness is always conscious of something: that is, it is directed towards things in everyday life. This consciousness intends towards something from the position of "I" (the first person singular, me). I am conscious of things in the world and am aware that others may be also, from their respective "I" positions, but it is "I" (of me) that apprehends my everyday life, knowing that others do so as well. Finally, it is said that, in my apprehending of the world, I do so in terms of zones of relevance. The closest zone to me is that which I am directly involved in, is easily accessible to me and is open to my influence and manipulation. Further out are other zones that are less accessible to me, that I have little interest in and only partial influence over. The furthest zone of relevance to me is that which is not accessible to me. I have no influence over it and my interest in it is merely potential: that is, I may one day be able to have some manipulation within it. Thus, the reality of everyday life is perceived by me, as well as by others (Schutz, 1970).

Social Interaction

We share the world with others, and we experience these others in different ways. "The most important experience of others takes place in the face-to-face situation, which is the prototypical case of social interaction. All other cases are derivatives of it" (Berger & Luckman, 1967, p. 43). This

The Social Construction of Stigma

face-to-face situation is shared with each other and, as I apprehend the other, thus he apprehends me. We are in a prime "I and Thou" relation that dominates our experience (Buber, 1922/1937). Although I know more about me, my history and my memory than I do about the other, the face-to-face situation remains dominant. This is because there is a constant interchange of expressivity between us as we interact. I smile, he smiles; I frown, he stops smiling; and so on. All my expressions are oriented towards him and all his to me. It is true that we may misinterpret expressions; nevertheless, it is only here in the face-to-face situation that the other's subjectivity is emphatically "close". Berger & Luckman claim that all other forms of relating to the other are, in varying degrees, "remote". In my interaction with the other, what he is is available to me as I focus on him. However, what "I" am is not quite so available to me, as I must stop and reflect on what "I" am to make it available to me. Thus, what the other is in the face-to-face situation is continuous and pre-reflective.

As I interact with the other in a face-to-face situation, I apprehend him by means of typificatory schemes. For example, I may apprehend the other as "an American", "a good guy", "a fool", "a drug addict", etc., and all these typifications will influence how my interaction will continue. Similarly, the other is also engaged in typifying me and a sort of ongoing negotiation of typificatory schemes continues throughout. Furthermore, typificatory schemes can be negotiated at a pre-arranged level, as in a bargaining process between buyer and seller. Thus, encounters with others in everyday life are typical in two senses; the other is apprehended as a type and the situation itself may be typical. Typifications of social encounters become progressively more anonymous the further away they are from the face-to-face situation, although they do continue. This means that when I apprehend the other in a face-to-face encounter I may, although I also may not, turn my attention to other contemporaries who are not in the face-to-face situation. "Anonymity increases as I go from the former [face-to-face] to the latter [not face-to-face], because the anonymity of the typifications by means of which I apprehend fellowmen in face-to-face situations is constantly 'filled in' by the multiplicity of vivid symptoms referring to a concrete human being" (Berger & Luckman, 1967, p. 47). Although there are obvious differences in my experiences of contemporaries in the world, it is the extent of anonymity or "closeness" that will influence how I typify them. This appears to be a basis for the stigmatisation process, whereby "the Black", "the White", "the Hindu", "the Muslim", "the Catholic", "the Protestant", "the disabled", and so on, become typified. Social reality is thus constructed through a continuous scheme of typifications that become progressively more anonymous the further away they are from the "here and now" of the face-to-face situation. Berger & Luckman (1967, p. 48) sum this up succinctly: "Social structure is the sum total of these typifications and of the recurrent patterns of interaction established by means of them. As such, social structure is an essential element of the reality of everyday life".

Language and Knowledge

Language and knowledge lie at the heart of social constructionism and the central theme to be dealt with concerns human expressivity. Human expression can be objectified, by which means both the producer and the recipient can share a common understanding. This is achieved through products of human activity that are available to all in the shared experience. For example, we can all recognise the bodily indices of the subjective experience of anger through facial expressions, posture, shaking fists, etc., and through verbal signs which might include hissing, grunting, screaming, etc. Once outside the face-to-face situation, the physical and verbal signs dissipate. However, the human expression of anger can be transmitted through a sign system. For example, if the angry person leaves an axe buried in my dining-room table or paints a skull and crossbones sign on my front door, they express their feeling of anger to me and to anyone else that may see them. Language itself can be defined as a system of vocal signs and is recognised as the most important sign system of human society (Berger & Luckman, 1967). Language is rooted in the here and now, but can be detached from it when one is shouting across a distance, speaking on the phone or radio, or even when writing (a second degree sign system). In the face-to-face situation, language shares a synchrony with both parties, speaker and listener, as at almost the same instance the speaker speaks and the listener listens to what is being spoken. Furthermore, language is capable of transcending the reality of everyday life and can span discrete spheres of reality. For example, it can interpret the meaning of a dream and explain it linguistically in our wide-awake world.

Language builds up semantic areas or zones of meaning for us that are circumscribed in a linguistic sense, and marks out coordinates of relevance for us. These fields are determined by our geographical and historical experience and, of course, differ for each individual. What is relevant to one person may not be relevant to another. This accumulation of relevant semantic fields constitutes what is known as our social stock of knowledge and includes both what is known and the limitations of that knowledge. The social stock of knowledge differentiates everyday reality through degrees of familiarity, as there are areas of life in which many people are extremely knowledgeable and other areas that they know very little about. It is the social stock of knowledge that provides the information for the process of typification that is undertaken routinely in everyday life. One event or situation, including the meeting of a person, is searched for in the social stock of knowledge to establish if it, or they, are typical of a previous experience or encounter, and this provides the basis of the potential response to it or them. Thus, if the social stock of knowledge only contains a negative experience of, say, meeting a sociologist and a situation occurs in which you are introduced to another sociologist, then this is likely to be typified as negative, all other things being equal.

Institutionalisation

All human activity has the potential to become habitualised. This patterning of behaviour is psychologically economical and will both reduce our need to deliberate on choices of action and free up our minds for new innovations. Remember, or imagine, the difficulties of learning to drive a car and attempting to coordinate the brakes, accelerator, clutch, gears, mirrors and steering. Yet very soon the process of driving becomes a habit, and most drivers do not need to concentrate on the intricacies of the driving procedures – though hopefully not to the level of being careless! Notwithstanding the dangerous aspects of this example, we can see that the habitualisation of this action reduces our choices in the way that we drive as, over time, we come to drive the way that we do, and this allows us to think about other things as we drive. Importantly, the meanings attached to this habitualised behaviour are retained and become embedded as routines in our general stock of knowledge. It is not only human behaviour, such as driving a car or dressing in the morning, that becomes habitualised, but also social interactions, such as greetings and departures, having tea or coffee with another, or attending a football match as a hooligan. These human actions become valued to both ourselves and the significant others in the social group to which we belong. Habitualisation precedes institutionalisation.

The vast amount of our human experience passes into our subconscious or unconscious minds and only a very small amount is held in our consciousness. If this were not the case, we would soon become "frozen" in inaction. Human experience, as it occurs, soon becomes sedimented in our recollections as memories, and we recognise these as our biography, as well as those of others as their history. Inter-subjective sedimentation occurs when an experience has been objectified in a sign system, predominantly a linguistic one, and only when this occurs can the meaning that it is endowed with be transmitted to others: i.e., the next generation. This becomes the basis of tradition. For example, both the hunting and the anti-hunting lobbies hold their traditions as valuable, with the "experience" of hunting being inter-subjectively sedimented. This is despite the fact that few in either group would actually have the basic experience of hunting for survival in its true sense, or of being hunted themselves. A bond is formed within both groups, based on the sedimented experiences embedded in the traditions of previous generations. These transmitted sedimentations are institutionalised and lead to those with their respective values performing a role in accordance with those beliefs: i.e., the hunters dress up and ride horses, with hounds and horns, and the anti-hunters engage in behaviours that are designed to try to stop them. We would not expect that a member of one of these groups would act in accordance with the beliefs of the other, although this may be both wished for and striven for. If these sedimented experiences, values and traditions involve what we may consider to be prejudice and stigma, then we can now appreciate how they become institutionalised within groups in society.

Legitimation

It would be rare for someone to state that they are prejudiced, that their belief system may be false, that their behaviour is discriminatory or that their actions are wrong; however, such insightful revelation would be the most important step on the road to change. Legitimation is the process by which the chances of this self-reflection are curtailed and Berger & Luckman (1967) refer to it as a second-order objectification of meaning. By this, they mean that legitimation produces new meanings, which incorporate the original meanings already formed from the institutionalisation processes. The second-order meanings are integrated into the first-order meanings to form a totality of meaning as an overall symbolic structure. These are referred to as symbolic universes. As Berger & Luckman (1967, p. 113) state: "These are bodies of theoretical tradition that integrate different provinces of meaning and encompass the institutional order in a symbolic totality". This allows us to appreciate symbolic universes such as "the police", "the army" and "the hospital". In taking the term "the police" as an example, we can see that it clearly comprises thousands of individuals who learn and operate the rules of policing. However, we can also appreciate "the police" as a single entity, in the sense of "That is what 'the police' do" or "That's 'the police' for you". "The police" in Britain are often said to be institutionally racist and we should now be in a position to see how this tradition, if it is true, is maintained. For this to become legitimated within "the police", the individual practices must become absorbed as a total overall symbolic universe into that which becomes known as "What 'the police' are". Legitimation governs the here and now and also governs the institution through its collective history. In social constructionist terms, this explains why such negative practices as institutional racism are perpetuated; but it also explains why positive practices are maintained. We will now move on to focus more closely on the second strand of our chapter, and that is a brief outline of some of the major writers on stigma.

Stigma

In its simplest sense, stigma is concerned with some form of mark that carries a disgrace and has negative connotations attached to it. Stigmata may be attached to a circumstance, quality or person, and has its Christian heritage in the marks on Christ's body following the crucifixion. There have been many writers on stigma, from many disciplines such as philosophy, theology and anthropology, and the five that we are about to outline are those that we consider to be the most relevant to our work on stigma in health care settings.

Foucault

Michel Foucault, the French intellectual, philosopher and historian of ideas, produced a central thesis on the notion of difference in his work *Madness and Civilisation* (1961/1967). Foucault argued that stigma had its etymological roots in religion, not only by referring to the marks of the crucifixion, but more importantly by marking out a difference. He suggested that early Christian society required the identification of difference based on that between those in God's favour and those who had fallen out of His good grace. Those that were considered to have fallen from favour were afflicted with a mark to identify them, and this mark, according to Foucault, was leprosy. He developed the thesis that, during the first ten centuries after the birth of Christ, leprosy defined difference through this highly visible mark from God and this allowed all manner of actions to be delivered to those with this condition. Throughout Europe at this period, leprosy was rife and lepers were colonised in lazar houses. Lazar refers to a poor and diseased person and, in particular, a leper. Over centuries, through the forced process of colonisation, leprosy in Europe was eventually eradicated. Foucault argues that this purge left a moral vacuum in society, whereby the difference between "them" (those out of God's favour) and "us" (those in God's favour) could no longer be seen via the mark of leprosy. Such a lack of a visible difference is threatening to society and could lead to all manner of fractures to the social bond. This appears closely related to a type of knowledge mentioned above and forms a reality for those involved.

For Foucault, the creation of difference through a visible sign was central to the idea of creating a "them" and an "us", which makes "us" feel safe. The lack of a "them" is threatening, as those out of God's favour cannot be identified amongst "us". This leads to social paranoia, as seen in witch-hunts, and accusations abound, damaging social ties. Foucault argued that, following the purge of leprosy, the social vacuum that was created was filled by madness. The lazar houses across Europe were filled by the mentally ill. Whereas, prior to this, madness was a community affair, popularly seen in terms of the "village idiot", the mentally ill now began to be excluded from society as the new "them". They were forced into colonies, which later became institutions, and in effect forced on to a

The Social Construction of Stigma

"journey". Foucault made good use of this notion of "journey" and employed Hieronymus Bosch's famous painting of the "Ship of Fools" (ca. 1494) as a symbol representing the idea of the mentally ill of that time being put on to ships to sail the canals of Europe. The ships were constantly in motion, moving "the problem" on to the next village or town in a perpetual movement. For Foucault, once they embarked on their "journey", there was no point of disembarkation and we can see much of modern psychiatry in these terms. For many patients with mental health problems, once they engage with modern psychiatric services, they are forced on a journey of "cure", from which they may never disembark.

Becker

Putting to one side simplistic notions of deviance, essentially based on the statistical definition of that which deviates from a norm or average, Howard Becker (1963) incorporated certain social elements into the concept. Becker's work on deviance is closely allied to stigma, as he also shelved the notion of the pathology of deviance as correlating to "diseased" as opposed to "healthy". He also disliked the sociological model of deviance, which predominantly saw some elements of society as promoting stability ("functional"), whilst others promoted instability ("dysfunctional"). He believed that society comprised many groups and sub-groups of people, each having their own sets of rules and sanctions for any transgressions. Individuals could belong to many different groups and could function within them, even though they might well be at odds with their values. For example, a person could belong to a respectable organisation and could also belong to a group of football hooligans. Members of any group who transgress the rules of that group are not a homogenous set, but merely deviant within the rule structure of the group to which they belong. Thus, the members of the group identify what it is that will be stigmatised. For the gang of football hooligans, it may be that to show compassion for an injured victim is a deviation from the norm of the group and that this will therefore be stigmatised accordingly. This, again, is the reality of everyday life.

Becker defined deviance in terms of how it was constructed by the social groups that formed the rules whose infraction constituted what they considered to be deviant. Becker puts it this way: "From this point of view, deviance is *not* a quality of the act that a person commits, but rather a consequence of the application by others of rules and sanctions to an 'offender'. The deviant is one to whom that label has successfully been applied; deviant behaviour is behaviour that people so label" (1963, p. 9). Becker's work located deviance at a social level and claimed that various media communications were part of this social character. Once so labelled, deviant groups also developed certain mechanisms of a social character to reinforce and maintain their status. These included such concepts as common fate, rationalising their position, self-justifying strategies, and a history on which to pin their experiences. Although Becker used the deviant behaviour of using marijuana as an example of deviancy, we can substitute any of the socially recognised stigmatising conditions in our society; for example, HIV/AIDS.

Goffman

Ervin Goffman, in his seminal book *Stigma: Notes on the Management of Spoiled Identity* (1963), defined stigma in terms of our personal knowledge of the person before us. He stated that: "While the stranger is present before us, evidence can arise of his possessing an attribute that makes him different from others in the category of persons available for him to be, and of a less desirable kind – in the extreme a person who is quite thoroughly bad, or dangerous, or weak. He is thus reduced in our minds from a whole and usual person to a tainted one. Such an attribute is a stigma" (p. 12). He outlined three different types of stigma: first, abominations of the body, such as various physical deformities; second, blemishes of individual character, which may be perceived as including weakness of will, being domineering, having unnatural passions, treacherousness, holding rigid beliefs and dishonesty; and third, the tribal stigmas of race, nation and religion. Although Goffman's text remains central to any work on stigma, he has been criticised as presenting too narrow a version. For example, Page (1984) argues that "physical deformities" is too restrictive in terms of suggesting deprivation pertaining to congenital abnormalities or malformations of human structures. Similarly, "blemishes of individual character" suggests a behavioural manifestation and Page argues that the term "conduct" more suitably fits this dimension of stigma.

Notwithstanding these criticisms, Goffman's understanding of stigma locates it from the viewpoint of society and shows how the individual can emerge socially as different. His concern with appreciating how and why some members of society choose to stigmatise a particular social group is important, as it also focuses on the perceptions of the stigmatised themselves. Thus, he identifies a relationship between those that stigmatise and those that are stigmatised. The tension that is created within this relationship is easily noted when a physically deformed person walks down the street; either he is stared at as a spectacle or eyes are quickly averted. Both responses lock both individuals into a self-reinforcing process of stigmatisation. There are a large number of vignettes in Goffman's text that are based on the personal experiences of stigmatised individuals and it is suggested that it is these personal accounts that ground the book in the life world of the marginalised "Other". He clearly sees stigma in terms of a two-way process, in which the stigmatising and the stigmatised are trapped in a value-laden course of interaction. It is interesting to note that, when the stranger (to be stigmatised) becomes known to us on a personal level, Goffman suggests that they largely become de-stigmatised. This resonates with our experiences in modern day society of racial and religious tensions between many groups of people who are not known to each other on a personal level. It also resonates with the grouping of people together, such as "the disabled"; our perceptions of them when we know the person as an individual alters, and this is closely associated with the notion of typification outlined above.

Jones, Farina, Hastorf, Markus, Miller, & Scott

Edward Jones and his co-workers produced a text, from a social psychology perspective, entitled *Social Stigma: The Psychology of Marked Relationships* (1984). Using different language to Goffman, they stated that: "We intend to focus in this book on a particular category of social relationships – those in which one participant has a condition that is at least potentially discrediting. We shall be concerned with the cognitive and affective underpinnings of such relationships and with the behavioural problems they entail. We shall also be concerned with the course and development of such relationships over time" (p. 6). This focused the work on the relationship between societal values and the perceptions of the marginalised individual as a devalued person. Therefore, it is concerned with the

The Social Construction of Stigma

feeling of stigma as perceived by vulnerable individuals, which in this context deals with personal responses, such as fear, anger, worthlessness, depression, etc. The emotional impact of these engendered feelings, whether or not explicitly evoked by societal responses to the stigmata, is implicitly felt as a corollary of those social expectations. The result of this, according to Jones et al., is the development of a mental strategy to deal with the social implications of the stigma. These were termed the "six dimensions".

These dimensions were, first, *concealability*, which refers to the extent to which the stigmata can be hidden and deals with the questions of to what extent its visibility is controllable or the wish to control it desirable. Clearly, a facial disfigurement is difficult to hide unless the person becomes socially isolated, and an unwanted pregnancy can only be hidden until the growing abdomen reveals its presence. The second dimension is *course*, which is concerned with the pattern of change in relation to social expectations of the stigmatised condition and examines what the anticipated social consequences of the outcome are. For example, with a terminal illness, there are a set of social relations that surround the person as they move towards their death which will affect conversations, particularly regarding the future. Third, *disruptiveness*, which refers to the extent to which the condition blocks or hampers either the social interaction of the stigmatised person or their communication with the social network: stigmatised conditions do affect the social network to one degree or another, and will govern what that person does and who they do it with. The fourth dimension refers to *aesthetic qualities*, which involves the signs and symbols of the condition that make the possessor repellent, ugly or upsetting. Burns, amputations, facial disfigurements, etc., may evoke a negative reaction in the perceiver, whilst more hidden conditions do not, and this creates an emotional reaction. Fifth is *origin*, which refers to the aetiology of the circumstances that led to the stigmatised condition in relation to the accounting of blame and involves identifying who holds responsibility for it. If the responsibility for a condition can be located as the person themselves, then they are more likely to be stigmatised for it. The final dimension is *peril*, which refers to the extent to which the condition poses any social danger and, if so, how imminent or serious it is. For example, a person with HIV/AIDS may be stigmatised as posing a social danger, as the perception is one of contagion. Again, we can see in the work of Jones et al. that stigma is centrally a social construction, through these six dimensions.

Scambler

Graham Scambler, writing in the UK, has made, and continues to make, a significant contribution to our understanding of stigma. The personal anxieties concerning stigmatised people's attempts to cope with their conspicuous positions in society is enlightened by his identification of *enacted* and *felt* stigma. Focusing his work on epilepsy, Scambler claims that enacted stigma produces very profound and damaging experiences when the person with epilepsy recalls being discriminated against. Enacted stigma refers to the stigmatised person being identified as such and then living the experience of stigmatisation. They are, in effect, "outed" and then live according to the expectations that society has of them. Scambler argues that the powerful force of the label "epileptic" creates a pattern of expectations, which the person then lives by. Felt stigma, on the other hand, refers to the shame that the person feels towards being associated with the diagnosis "epileptic". Furthermore, there is a fear of being

The Social Construction of Stigma

discriminated against simply on the grounds of this label and Scambler goes on to state that "the sense of felt stigma is so strong that people with epilepsy typically do their utmost to maintain secrecy about their symptoms and the diagnostic label: they disclose only when it strikes them as prudent or necessary" (1997, p. 176). We can see that keeping the label hidden would reduce the likelihood of encountering enacted stigma, but we can also see that felt stigma would be more disruptive to the lives of the stigmatised.

Scambler has examined a number of medical conditions that create stigmatisation, and these include rectal cancer, HIV/AIDS, psoriasis and severe burns. Analysing these conditions in the framework of health and illness, he shows how these "stigmatising conditions can be defined as conditions that set their possessors apart from 'normal' people, that mark them as socially unacceptable or inferior beings" (1997, p. 187). Illness involves deviance and stigma on two levels. Firstly, by the individual deviating from the social norm and being labelled as "sick"; and secondly, by having a condition that is socially uncomfortable to the remainder of society. These conditions, and there are many more, inevitably require contact with the medical professionals who are attempting to provide a quality care service, and the encounter with these health professionals is crucial in the stigmatising process. We will now look at a number of examples of this in health care settings.

Health Care Settings

Health care settings are communities with characteristics that in some fundamental and profound way set them apart from the rest of society. They are places where vulnerable, injured, damaged and hurt members of society intersect with professional people, whose purpose is to aid, assist and care for them. These settings can embrace any social situation in which those who have a health care need are administered some form of medical attention, in its all-inclusive sense. Outside the home, these can range from a General Practitioner's surgery to a field hospital in a war zone. All of those people who need this medical attention present some vulnerable attribute, which has tarnished their image of themselves in some way. The vulnerability of patients in health care settings, because of their "difference", all too frequently leads to their being subject to and experiencing stigmatisation both from the wider society and from the health care professionals.

It should be remembered that the impact and force of stigmas change over time. Our prejudicial views alter according to our social norms, which are rooted in the particular period of history in which we are living. For example, in the 1980s the gay community suffered an onslaught of the stigmatisation process. Of course, the gay community has always felt excluded and alienated to varying degrees, but the HIV/AIDS epidemic brought a resurgence of stigma from the wider society. Stigma, of whatever origin, is rooted in fear and this fear all too frequently stems from an ignorance of the "affliction". As society's knowledge base of HIV/AIDS has developed, and as it is no longer a disease that exclusively targets homosexuals, society's moral panic has somewhat fallen. We are, in theory at least, a society which is becoming more integrated, and as those people with potential and anticipated stigmatising conditions, as described by Scambler (1997), increasingly live and work in mainstream society, their experiences of being stigmatised should fall (Goffman, 1963; Whitehead, 2001). We will now discuss three areas of stigmatisation in health care settings and, despite their unique characteristics, they illustrate a number of fundamental properties that are common to all stigmas.

The Stigma of Congenital Abnormalities

Farrell & Corrin (2001) outline the case of stigma and congenital abnormalities. They begin their chapter with the historical impact of stigma in relation to congenital abnormalities and show how this has changed over time. For example, in early Greek times congenital abnormalities were seen as a sign of divine retributive intervention for sins committed in a previous life, and in early Roman civilisation there is some evidence that statutes existed which instructed the head of the family to kill their child if it was born with a deformity. Furthermore, in medieval and Tudor times, babies born with congenital abnormalities were seen as *changelings*: that is, the devil's substitutes for human children. We are also told that Martin Luther, the Protestant reformer, considered the disabled child to be the devil incarnate and recommended terminating the baby's life.

The authors go on to discuss the great expectations that surround the impending birth of a child, with the many social interactions that accompany it and create an air of anticipation at this time. The shattering of these expectations is profound if the baby is born with a congenital abnormality, and the reactions of professionals, then of parents, and then of the social network, reinforce negative perceptions of the deformity. At the point of birth, the two main questions that parents ask are (a) "Is it a boy or a girl?" and (b) "Is it alright?" Professionals, doctors and midwives who are unable to respond positively to the latter question are faced with the dilemma of how to answer and the inevitable hesitancy and avoidance begin the process of stigmatisation. Parents lose their prime expectation of a "healthy baby" and give way to a perception of weakness, vulnerability and pity. Their self-image as "good parents" is challenged and leads to intense psychological trauma. Parental feelings range from ambivalence to revulsion in the aftermath of this. The social network is altered, as some family members and social friends become hesitant at approaching a family with a child with an abnormality, as they do not know what to say or do. Many parents of a child born with such a deformity may seek the company of others in a similar situation, often in the form of support groups. In any event, the social network is altered, and there are many reports of awkward encounters in social settings when a baby with congenital abnormalities is thrust upon an unsuspecting stranger.

Although modern-day surgery can correct or lessen the impact of such congenital abnormalities, it is often unhelpful to the parents to dismiss the deformity with unrealistic positive comments regarding the future. Although these are designed to help, they rarely do. Farrell & Corrin (2001) argue that stigma can be lessened by reflection, recognising the individuality of the child and the family, focusing on the personal attributes of the child, engaging in active listening and forming a therapeutic relations framework. Society sees the child with congenital abnormalities as a stranger, both in terms of being unknown and also deviating from the norm, and constructs a response to this, which is largely negative. Only by getting to "know" the child and its relation to the disability, and in turn its relation to society, can the stigma be overcome.

The Social Construction of Stigma

Teenage Pregnancy, Stigma and Differential Provision of Health Care

According to Jacono & Jacono (2001), teenage pregnancy is a major concern in most industrialised countries and, although it has long been considered "shameful" in Western society, its current "epidemic" is seen to have its roots in the "sexual revolution of the sixties". The concern alluded to here involves social, moral and financial issues. The rates of teenage pregnancy are on the increase, with half a million reported each year in the USA and 20 per 1000 teenage women giving birth in Britain (Jacono & Jacono, 2001). The social concerns surround the breakdown in social networks, as these teenagers lose an element of "freedom", and the high rates of divorce, leading to an increase in single parents becoming socially isolated. The moral issue has its roots deep in religious traditions, the family and the sanctity of sex within marriage; those seen to have "succumbed" being deemed to have fallen from God's grace. The financial issues largely involve the fact that approximately half of all teenage pregnant women go on welfare in the USA and 90% receive income support in Britain (Jacono & Jacono, 2001). There are, of course, other issues that are important for teenage pregnancies and these include higher death rates, lower birth weights and higher rates of psycho-physiological dysfunctions in the children of teenage mothers.

Stigmatisation occurs through a process of victimisation, as the teenager is considered to be morally "weak-willed" in not resisting the drives and urges of male advances and her own passions. She is considered to be inferior in not being able to wait until marriage and ignorant in not taking precautions. She is regarded as being responsible for her condition and is viewed as having to be fully accountable for her future. Whitehead (2001) argues that this leads to a form of "social death". Teenage pregnant women are perceived as having "loose morals" and of being "over-sexed" and they can be seen as a mark of shame for family and friends. Parental reactions may include anger, deep feelings of disgrace and betrayal, and may even lead to the abandonment of the daughter, who can become ostracised and isolated, especially if the father of the pregnant teenager is no longer in the relationship. As Jacono & Jacono (2001, p. 229) point out: "Since there appear to be no social, religious, economic or cultural boundaries that it does not cross, it generates a great deal of fear in those who perceive themselves (or their loved ones) to be at risk for becoming part of this group". Thus, the social construction of the stigma of teenage pregnancy is processed through the mediums of religion, family, parents and culture.

Breastfeeding

One does not automatically associate breastfeeding with stigma in the way that one would congenital abnormality or HIV/AIDS; however, Smale (2001) offers a sophisticated account of how this occurs in our society. There are cultural differences in breastfeeding in public, with Africa, Asia and Scandinavia largely accepting this practice, whilst in Britain it is largely unacceptable. In fact, Smale (2001) argues that breastfeeding in public in Britain appears to be less tolerated the further one travels from London, and she explains the process by which this natural practice becomes stigmatised. She focuses on two of the dimensions of Jones et al (1984), "origin" and "peril", to show how this occurs. The visible signs of the stigmata are the damp stains from the nipples and the possibility of the related smell; millions of pads are sold each year to manage this.

The Social Construction of Stigma

The possibility of let-down as the baby ceases suckling, with arching streams of milk squirting from the breasts, is a visible and embarrassing sign. Noises, such as the gulping of milk by a hungry baby, betray the passage of body fluids, and even silent, or discreet, breastfeeding may provoke reactions in others. Smale (2001) sees the dimension of peril and breastfeeding, not as a direct threat to others, but as a challenge to the social order. The production of bare breasts in our society is culturally disallowed, unless in certain defined areas such as when sunbathing on the beach, and the management of transfer from invisible breasts to a bare breast being suckled is particularly difficult for women with twins or with large breasts.

Smale (2001) gives us numerous accounts of women being asked not to feed their babies in public, being requested to go to the toilet to feed, being told it is "rude", revolting or disgusting, and that the expulsion of all body fluids from orifices should be done in private. Smale argues that, although most of us like to eat out and do not mind being in the presence of others eating out, this does not always extend to babies breastfeeding. She also highlights how language and silence are employed in the social construction of the stigma of breastfeeding. "Journalists have compared public breastfeeding to the siting of urinals in bars or vomitaria in restaurants, and to self-medication ("shooting up") by diabetics .... These powerful parallels reveal powerful meanings, just as the action of an irate shopkeeper – throwing dirty water over a mother and baby as they breastfed outside his shop – recalls that of someone separating copulating dogs" (p. 239). In this very powerful chapter, Smale reveals how this natural and benign activity can become stigmatised through the social construction of the breast as belonging to the domain of sex; thus, it should be kept hidden from public view.

Conclusions

We have been concerned throughout our work on stigma and social exclusion with how professional health care staff contribute towards the stigmatisation process and then perpetuate it in their practice. This is not to say that we believe that this process is often undertaken malevolently or deliberately, although occasionally this might well be so, but that it occurs unknowingly or inevitably. In this chapter, we have attempted to identify some of the major components of social constructionism, followed by a brief outline of the work of some of the major workers on stigma, and then highlighted three areas in which health care staff may contribute towards the stigmatisation of others. By employing these three areas, social constructionism, stigma and health care settings, we hope that we have gone some small way to revealing the complexity of a cultural mosaic that is constructed of many elements. The first involves the fact that we are first and foremost socialised individuals in the society to which we belong, long *before* we become professionalised members of our chosen discipline. Our professional values and ethics may well be at odds with our personal ones and create a tension and, although we may like to think that we can bracket off our personal views in order to operate with our professional ones, sometimes this fails. Furthermore, this situation is further compounded when we add to the analysis of the social dimension cultural values, which again may conflict with our personal and professional standards.

In conclusion, there are a number of measures that ought to be undertaken by all involved in the stigmatisation process, and not just health care professionals. The first, we would argue, is to reveal to ourselves our role in the process of stigmatisation and not to deny it. This requires a self-reflective approach to our thoughts and actions, and it can be a painful endeavour. However, it is fundamental to the change process. The second is to see people beyond a mere label and to "know" them as individuals. Empathy is required for us to be able to identify with them. Thirdly, we need to check our thoughts against our actions, to see if there is a contradiction between them and to establish if we are thinking and doing different things. Finally, for now, we should educate and train our professionals to identify areas in practice that are creating and maintaining stigma and to provide them with the skills and expertise to change this. Stigma, discrimination and prejudice have no place in a civilised society, and certainly no place in our health care services.

References

Becker, H. S. (1963). *Outsiders: Studies in the sociology of deviance.* London: Free Press of Glencoe.

Berger, P. L., & Luckman, T. (1967). *The social construction of reality: A treatise in the sociology of knowledge.* London: Allen Lane.

Buber, M. (1937). *I and thou* (R. G. Smith, Trans.). Edinburgh: T & T Clark. (Original work published 1922).

Descartes, R. (1968). *Discourse on method, and The meditations* (F. E. Sutcliffe, Trans.). Harmondsworth: Penguin. (Original works published 1637, 1641).

Durkheim, E. (1938). *The rules of sociological method* (S. A. Solovay & T. H. Mueller, Trans.; G. E. G. Catlin, Ed.). (8th ed.). Glencoe, IL: Free Press. (Original work published 1895).

Farrell, M., & Corrin, K. (2001). The stigma of congenital abnormalities. In T. Mason, C. Carlisle, C. Watkins, & E. Whitehead (Eds.), *Stigma and social exclusion in healthcare* (pp. 51-62). London: Routledge.

Foucault, M. (1967). *Madness and civilisation: A history of insanity in the age of reason* (R. Howard, Trans.). London: Tavistock. (Original work published 1961).

Foucault, M. (1970). *The order of things: An archaeology of the human sciences.* London: Tavistock. (Original work published 1966).

Goffman, E. (1963). *Stigma: Notes on the management of spoiled identity.* Englewood Cliffs, NJ: Prentice-Hall.

Jacono, J., & Jacono B. (2001). Teenage pregnancy, stigma and differential provision of healthcare. In T. Mason, C. Carlisle, C. Watkins, & E. Whitehead (Eds.), *Stigma and social exclusion in healthcare* (pp. 226-233). London: Routledge.

Jones, E. E., Farina, A., Hastorf, A. H., Markus, H., Miller, D. T., & Scott, R. A. (1984). *Social stigma: The psychology of marked relationships.* New York: W. H. Freeman.

Nachmias, C., & Nachmias, D. (1981). *Research methods in the social sciences.* (2nd ed.). New York: St. Martin's Press. (Original work published 1976).

Page, R. M. (1984). *Stigma.* London: Routledge & Kegan Paul.

Plato. (1977). *The republic* (D. Lee, Trans.). 2nd ed. Harmondsworth: Penguin. (Original ed. of this translation, 1955).

Scambler, G. (1997). Deviance, sick-role and stigma. In G. Scambler, (Ed.), *Sociology as applied to medicine* (pp. 171-181). (4th ed.). London: W. B. Saunders.

Schutz, A. (1970). *On phenomenology and social relations* (H. R. Wagner, Ed.). Chicago. University of Chicago Press.

Smale, M. (2001). The stigmatisation of breastfeeding. In T. Mason, C. Carlisle, C. Watkins, & E. Whitehead (Eds.), *Stigma and social exclusion in healthcare* (pp. 234-245). London: Routledge.

Social Exclusion Unit. (1998). *Truancy and social exclusion: Report.* London: Stationery Office.

Social Exclusion Unit. (1999). *Review of the Social Exclusion Unit.* London: Author.

Social Exclusion Unit. (2000). *Young people: Report by Policy Action Team 12 [for the] National Strategy for Neighbourhood Renewal.* London: Stationery Office.

Weber, M. (1947) *The theory of social and economic organization* (A. M. Henderson & T. Parsons, Trans.; T. Parsons, Ed.). New York: Free Press. (Original work published 1921).

Whitehead, E. (2001). Teenage pregnancy: On the road to social death. *International Journal of Nursing Studies, 38,* 437-446.

5

CLASS AND INEQUALITY IN CONTEMPORARY BRITAIN

Mike Savage

In this chapter, I give an overview of my research on class and equality in Britain, framing it around the debate about whether we are currently seeing new forms of structural inequality in Britain or whether we are seeing forms of social exclusion. Certainly, if you look at policy debates today, there is a commonly held view which says that we have moved away from a society based upon structural inequality towards a society in which there are forms of social exclusion. These exclusions are often seen as affecting only particular types of people with specific kinds of problems. However, if we think about class and inequality seriously, that view becomes untenable and forces us to realise that inequality is still a fundamental feature of our society. Such structural inequality is of a very complex form, however, and this is the paradox I want to unravel. The paradox of class, as I call it, is that, in terms of material inequalities, class is an ever more powerful determinant of our lives, our housing, our health and our income. Yet, at the same time, people do not seem very consciously aware of class as something which is meaningful to them. And so there is a kind of paradox whereby, just as class is in fact extremely important to us, we find it difficult to talk about it and recognise it.

Decoding Discrimination

The chapter begins with a discussion of different ways of thinking about inequality and particularly of trying to differentiate the idea of social exclusion from the idea of social inequality. Then, in the second part of the chapter, I will discuss a few issues surrounding class polarisation in Britain, how it is increasing and how it has increased in the last twenty years. That is one part of the paradox: at one level, a structural level, we are seeing ever more social divisions. But then, in parts three and four, I will focus upon the other aspect of the paradox, which is the non-recognition of class; that is, if you actually ask people about whether or not they feel proud about belonging to a class or if they feel they belong to a social class, then most people give hesitant responses and do not consciously have a very strong sense of class awareness. I will discuss this in the context of some research that I have been doing over the last three or four years, during the course of which I interviewed people living around Manchester, asking them among other things what they thought about class and whether or not they thought they were members of a social class.

Finally, I will examine an issue which, though of extreme importance, has not at the moment really been picked up by the media. There is currently a great concern in our society about falling levels of political and social participation, the recognition that people's lifestyles are becoming increasingly private, and that people are less likely to join voluntary associations or get involved in charity work than was the case twenty or thirty years ago. In this section, I intend to illustrate that what is actually happening is that working class people are dropping out of political and social life. They are becoming more fatalistic and more detached from forms of social and political participation, so that in many respects we are seeing a kind of unstated middle class norm dominate much of our public life. This is frequently not recognised, but it is something which poses great problems for encouraging the integration and the participation of all groups in our society in any kind of equal way.

Thinking about Inequality

Of great importance in recent debates about social inclusion and exclusion has been the idea that we are now living in a classless society. Famously, Margaret Thatcher said in the 1980s that we were a society of individuals; that there is no such thing as society, there are only individuals and their families. Politicians like her successor, John Major, who said that we were living in a classless society, continued that rhetoric. Tony Blair and "New Labour" have also echoed the idea that we are no longer living in a society characterised by fundamental class inequalities. The New Labour Government has been important in developing a kind of policy shift in terms of thinking about inequality, by arguing that, rather than thinking about structured class inequality, which used to be something that the Labour Party took very seriously (or fairly seriously), we are now living in a society in which the majority of people are part of a kind of middle mass, an included group. The problem of exclusion is one that still exists, as there are pockets of people who are still disadvantaged, but their problems can be resolved by specific policy initiatives. So, inequality is not being seen as a fundamental feature of society, but as something more contingent. Therefore, the implications of this type of New Labour policy is that, for most people, inequality is not an issue, because most people form part of a comfortably-off middle class, which would include 70% or 80% of the population. Insofar as problems still exist, forms of exclusion can be found, but these tend to affect only specific people for particular reasons: single parents, the long-term unemployed, the disabled, and so on. There is no major group in society, such as the working class, that is still structurally and systematically disadvantaged, and so the implication of current political discourse, which arguably is to some extent shared by all three major political parties, is that the core structure of our modern society is basically acceptable.

This view of social inequality is fundamentally different from the view which sociologists have propounded over the years. Without wishing to spend too much time talking about the sociological view, it would be useful to consider some familiar interpretations. If we think about Marx's interpretation of society, he sees a contradiction, a conflict between capital and labour, between the middle class and the working class, as being fundamental. That is not something that you can actually eliminate without changing the whole fabric of our society. Even though Max Weber is often seen as arguing a different case about class from Marx, he also thought that the competition for resources was fundamental to social life. He also saw inequality based around different market positions, different market assets being a fundamental feature of all modern societies. Although he did not see a straightforward division between middle and working class or capital and labour as Marx did, he still saw inequality and a kind of striving for self-advancement in modern society as being a fundamental feature and a fundamental cause of social disharmony and social conflict. More recently, Pierre Bourdieu has perhaps been the most important thinker in arguing that in all modern societies we see a fundamental power that he calls cultural capital. Those people with cultural resources and appropriate cultural backgrounds have the systematic power to undercut and undermine the cultures of those who form part of the working class. Bourdieu is not only concerned with the economic nature of inequality, but also with the way in which privileged groups are culturally entitled and use their cultural entitlement subtly - or not so subtly – to keep working class groups in their place. We will return to Bourdieu's arguments in the course of this chapter, since they have a great deal of subtle power in terms of understanding the nature of contemporary society.

Class and Inequality in Britain

Whatever the rhetoric about classlessness, the reality is that over the last twenty years we have seen a steady widening of income levels between those people who are in the top 30% or 40% of the population and those people who are beneath that. Historically, the period when we had most equality in Britain was the 1970s. It was in that decade that the (Labour) government set up a Royal Commission on the Distribution of Income and Wealth, which suggested that the incomes of top earners should be capped and that the incomes of those at the bottom should be boosted. The pay policies of that decade, under a Labour government and the "Social Contract", were designed to give higher proportional wage increases to those at the bottom of the income distribution scale. It is unimaginable that a government today - whether Labour or Conservative - would seriously attempt to interfere with the pay levels of the top earners. It is now seen as a process that is driven fundamentally by market features. We have had an interesting case recently with respect to fire fighters, in which that principle has been tested. The point is that we are seeing a situation in which attempts by governments to encourage equality have been given up and instead we are seeing a steady widening of pay differentials.

Decoding Discrimination

We could consider this in many ways, but the following table gives a flavour of the basic trends. It compares the pay of men and women in 1991 and 1998:

Facets of income by occupational group, 1991-1998
(*Source:* New Earnings Survey [1991, 1998])

MEN   1991

Occupational group	% deviation from national average	40-9 as index of average	Top decile as index of median
Managers	40.4	112	192
Professionals	34.1	108	159
Associate professionals	17.5	111	175
Clerical	-25.7	116	162
Craft	-14.5	109	150
Personal services	-14.6	117	151
Sales	-13.8	119	173
Plant operatives	-20.0	108	156
Other	-31.2	109	161

MEN   1998

Occupational group	% deviation from national average	40-9 as index of average	Top decile as index of median
Managers	46.4	110	197
Professionals	33.0	106	166
Associate professionals	20.8	108	180
Clerical	-31.7	111	155
Craft	-15.6	109	164
Personal services	-20.5	121	162
Sales	-20.5	120	184
Plant operatives	-22.1	107	164
Other	-34.3	105	164

Class and Inequality in Contemporary Britain

WOMEN   **1991**

Occupational group	% deviation from national average	40-9 as index of average	Top decile as index of median
Managers	32.0	100	180
Professionals	51.2	102	132
Associate professionals	24.9	109	148
Clerical	-11.8	102	153
Craft	-28.4	103	170
Personal services	-22.3	102	164
Sales	-23.6	100	169
Plant operatives	-25.6	103	150
Other	-33.0	101	159

WOMEN   **1998**

Occupational group	% deviation from national average	40-9 as index of average	Top decile as index of median
Managers	40.6	102	182
Professionals	48.1	101	138
Associate professionals	21.4	105	147
Clerical	-16.8	102	149
Craft	-29.7	98	165
Personal services	-28.9	102	169
Sales	-25.4	98	186
Plant operatives	-26.2	102	154
Other	-37.6	101	165

These figures indicate whether or not a particular group earns more or less than the national average. If there is a minus figure it means it is below the national average, if it is a plus figure it means it is above the national average.

Decoding Discrimination

My main point is really a very simple one. There are three groups who earn above the national average for men and women: managers (i.e. of industries in the private and public sector); professionals (i.e. doctors, lawyers, etc.); and associate professionals (i.e. people like nurses). The basic point is that an individual earning more than the national average in 1991 would be earning even more than the national average in 1998. The salaries of managers who earned 40% above the national average for men in 1991 had gone up to 46% more than that average by 1998. Conversely, those earning less than the national average in 1991 were earning even less than the national average in 1998. There is only one exception to that, which I think is an interesting one. This is for some professionals, whose pay levels are being basically capped at about one-third above the national average. These professionals, of course, mainly work in the public sector and are affected by public sector economic policies; but, leaving them aside, it is particularly true that those people earning beneath the national average, such as clerical workers, craft workers, personal service workers, sales workers, plant workers, etc., have in every case suffered a proportionate decline in earnings. This is true for both women and men. If we trace these statistics back into the early 1980s, which is difficult because the basis of occupational classification has changed, we would find the same trends taking place over the past twenty years. So we are seeing managers and associate professionals pulling ahead of average national income levels, while manual workers and routine white-collar workers, in particular, are left behind.

These figures are not really in doubt and the government recognises them. What are the reasons for them? There are three possible explanations for these differences. One of the arguments used by sociologists in the past to justify income inequalities was to say that society rewards those occupations which are held in the highest esteem. For instance, if we value the work of lawyers and doctors, then we tend to reward them highly. Conversely, if we do not think that the work of road sweepers or factory workers is very valuable, then we tend to give them the lowest pay. Whatever the theoretical limitations of this view, we can see that this explanation does not hold today, because actually managers are not held in particularly high esteem by the British population. If we were to ask people what kinds of jobs are sociably valuable, managers on the whole would not get a particularly high rating. Groups like nurses, professionals, and also some forms of manual work, for example fire fighters, get reasonably high esteem. Yet this does not seem to translate into levels of pay. There is actually very little correlation between the esteem in which a job is held and its level of pay.

Another explanation argues that skill and education are crucial. Those occupations which demand higher levels of skill are therefore paid higher, partly because there are fewer people who can do these jobs and partly as a kind of incentive for people to undergo the extensive training which is required. Again, there is some degree of truth in this, insofar as it is well known that the more qualified one is, the better income one can expect to earn. This is by no means a perfect correlation, however. What has been shown is that in some kinds of jobs, those which are seen as being part of a secondary labour market, one has very little chance of boosting one's pay, regardless of one's qualifications and skills. Therefore, for much of the clerical, factory and personal service sectors, having extra occupational qualifications does not increase employees' earnings to any great extent. Similarly, for some kinds of jobs in the professional sector, it is important to get qualifications, not because they necessarily provide the skills required, but simply because they give access to key jobs.

What these figures suggest – although we will not find this being talked about in government circles - is that we are seeing here the power of class. Put crudely, what we are seeing is the ability of top people to look after their own interests and to make sure that their own nests are feathered: to restructure and reorganise industry in such a way that the balance of power and inequality is shifted towards those at the top. The best examples of this process have undoubtedly been the privatisation of industry in the 1980s and the de-mutualisation of building societies in the 1980s and 1990s. A key element of these changes has been the way in which chief executives and managers have realised they can massively increase their own pay if they change from being either mutual or public sector bodies to being private sector bodies. Even outside these cases, we can see a very similar trend, whereby those holding senior positions are able to restructure, giving themselves increasing power and significance. It is absolutely clear that these inequalities have ramifications in all sorts of areas, including housing and health. One of the major embarrassments of health policy has been that, despite the restructuring of health services and increasing investment in them, relative class inequalities in health remain extremely persistent and show little sign of declining. The reality of these figures is that, fundamentally, nothing has changed, except in some cases for the worse. If we go back to the thinking of Marx, we can see that he predicted increasing class polarisation and he anticipated that this would lead to conflict, as people at the bottom of society recognised their position and tried to do something about it.

Class and Inequality in Contemporary Britain

The paradox of class

This leads on to the next point, which is that this restructuring of income does not really map in a very clear form on to people's perceptions of class. This is the paradox of class - even though class is of fundamental importance, people tend not to recognise it subjectively; they tend not to see it as an issue that they should feel concerned about. At their level of culture and awareness, therefore, class is actually of relatively muted significance. This is a fairly controversial point, which warrants further discussion.

It is true that, in Britain, the majority of people do know to which class they belong. When asked in surveys, over 90% of people will, if pressed, say that they do belong to a social class, and they split roughly half and half between saying they are working class or middle class, even though the majority of people no longer work in traditional manufacturing industries. This is actually rather unusual, as in most societies very few people say that they are working class and it is decidedly striking to have a proportion of between 50% and 60% of people saying that they are. However, although at one level research indicates that people do say they are members of a certain class, it is also the case that they often say that because they have been provoked by the interviewers into give themselves a class label. Actually, if we ask people in depth what they think about class, then it becomes clear that their sense of belonging to a class is ambivalent, muted and hesitant. In the research I did in Manchester with Gaynor Bagnall and Brian Longhurst (2005), we interviewed about 200 people; our interviews were not questionnaires, but in-depth interviews, which were tape-recorded, and we did not ask them about their sense of class until the end of the interview. We basically asked two questions. One of them was: "John Major argued that Britain is becoming a classless society. Do you agree with that?" We then asked, "Do you think of yourself as belonging to a social class?" We found out that the majority of people did not think we were becoming a classless society and would agree with the kind of account given a few minutes ago. However, when we asked if they themselves belonged to a social class, only about one third of people gave a clear, unequivocal answer and said, "Yes, I am working class", or, "Yes, I am middle class". About two thirds of people actually gave a rather ambivalent or hesitant answer: "Well, perhaps I am working class, but ...", or, "You know, I don't really think in terms of class, though you could say I am working class". These comments come from transcripts of the interviews that we did and provide a good example of how people dissociate from class.

We then asked, "If you had to describe yourself as any particular social class, what would you describe yourself as?" One person said, "Well middle class, working class/middle class, a bit of both", as if they are not actually that different, even though sociologists have often argued that there really is a very big difference between whether people see themselves as middle class or working class. Another person replied, "'I think, or I am, just me and this is how I am, take me or leave me". In other words, what matters to this woman is not that she is a member of a particular class, but that she is herself: a person, an individual. Another response was, "I don't feel very class conscious. Obviously, I am somewhere in the middle of lower middle class, I suppose, but I don't slot myself in to any particular group. I like to think that I am just me." When another woman was asked, "So you wouldn't see yourself as belonging to any particular social class?", she replied, "No, I am a postmaster's granddaughter, I have got no money", and continued, "I wouldn't see myself as any particular class. My grandfather used to reckon he was middle class and my father obviously was working class". When she was then asked, "Is this something that matters to you, i.e. class", she said "No"; but she went on to say that she was surprised to see how snobbish she was. A very common thing people said was, "I think it is important that we all treat people equally. It doesn't matter what your social background is, you can treat people the same. You can talk to people in the same way, regardless of whether they are a road sweeper or the prime minister". This sort of quotation could be duplicated. It seems that people can say that they are members of a certain social class, but it is not something that they feel very strongly about, and on the whole they try to dissociate themselves from class.

So, most people do not feel attached to a sense of class identity, and this is something that is very different from what Marx expected, when he thought people would become class conscious and rise up and challenge the system. Clearly, with a few exceptions (and there are some exceptions, particularly people who do have a sense of being members of the working class and feeling proud of it), on the whole people actually think that class is just a label; it is something out there, which market researchers, politicians, sociologists and so on use, but it is not something that actually means anything to them. Therefore, when they respond to surveys and say that they are middle class or working class, it is not something that is really salient to their sense of who they are, and therefore it is not really relevant to their sense of culture or their values. We should reflect on how sociologists in the past have made a great deal about the way in which some people define themselves as middle class and others as working class. Interestingly, some people used working class definitions and middle class definitions in the same interview. The reason for this seems to be that what matters to people is not that they belong to a class, but that they can emphasise that they are ordinary, normal people. They can try to do this in two ways. One of them is to say, "Well, if I am middle class, I must be in the middle. I am neither especially wealthy nor particularly poor". However, it is also possible to say, "Well, if I am working class, I am normal, because I work like everybody else". In this way, calling yourself middle class or working class are basically two ways of saying the same thing, which is that "I am just an ordinary person jogging along, there is nothing particularly unusual or different about me". The majority of people in our sample (90%) shared this sense that they neither wanted to see themselves as snobbish and elitist, nor as particularly badly off, but really as part of this kind of middle grouping in society.

In many respects, these views do reflect the rhetoric of social inclusion which the government has championed. So why is it the case that people do say these things? Two recent pieces of research have addressed this issue in interesting ways. Beverley Skeggs (1997) interviewed nearly a hundred women growing up in an old factory town in the North West that had fallen upon hard times. What she found out was that these working class women, who had had a particularly tough time, actually did not want to think about class, as it was too difficult, too dangerous and too frightening for them. Therefore, they dissimulated, preferring to claim that they were "respectable" or "feminine". The power of cultural capital means that people at the bottom of society do not want to think about class, because if they did it would be too threatening to their sense of identity. It is easier for them to try to sweep it under the carpet and pretend that it does not really exist. Similar conclusions in some ways are reached in *A Phenomenology of Working Class Experience* (2000), a study by Simon Charlesworth of mainly working class men in Rotherham, the South Yorkshire steel town which has also been very severely hit by the climate of the steel industry. The account he gives is of working class young men being completely without hope and cut off from society, but without the resources to think about things in terms of class. What both Charlesworth and Skeggs are doing is drawing upon the work of Bourdieu, and suggesting that what we are really seeing is the power of the culturally privileged middle classes to make the working class, the people without cultural capital, feel inadequate. This inadequacy then makes them experience and feel their problems in an individualised way, as something to do with themselves rather than with the nature of our society. These findings on the whole can be applied to the research we did in Manchester. There is a kind of awareness, when we talk about class, that it is a dangerous subject, and this leads respondents to say, "Well, I'm just me, you know" and to try to draw boundaries between themselves and society, in a way that is ultimately unattainable, as it is impossible. We are all profoundly affected by the society in which we live.

Civic Participation and Class

We also need to discuss participation in social life. What Charlesworth and Skeggs are pointing to is the way in which being working class is stigmatised; and one way of dealing with that stigma is to disidentify with it and say, "Well, we are not working class. Class is not important". This is related to current debates about what is happening in terms of people's social involvement in our society. There is now great concern about the fact that people are showing less interest in various forms of public activity.

For instance, people's trust in politicians is waning, people are less likely to vote than ever before and membership of political parties in Britain is haemorrhaging and collapsing. Both the Conservative and Labour Parties have seen their membership halve over a fifteen-year period. This worrying trend means that, unless membership can be boosted, all three main parties are going to be staffed by a very small number of people. This links in to some very high profile debates in the USA, which have been fuelled by the work of a political scientist called Robert Putnam (2000). He asserts that there is a long-term process in our society towards what he calls civic disengagement. Fifty years ago, he argues, in any American small town there would have been a whole web of activities, with a host of voluntary associations and many people being regular church-goers; in other words, a very active public realm in which people were socially and civically engaged. People would have been very reactive neighbours, looking after old people down the street, and there was a very strong sense of belonging to a community. He argues that, if we look at trends in American society over the last fifty years, we now see that those forms of civic engagement are falling apart, and he has some particularly powerful evidence concerning the falling numbers of members of various forms of clubs and associations from virtually every kind of organisation in the USA. This trend towards falling membership has developed over the last fifty years, even though people are now more likely to be well-educated and therefore, it might be supposed, more predisposed towards involvement in voluntary associations.

Putnam remarks that this change is to do with a number of factors. It is partly to do with people living more private lives and not bothering to go out and make social contacts, and partly to do with TV and the growing trend for them to get all their information and contacts from the mass media. Furthermore, he thinks that it is partly to do with women going out to work and there being less stable home lives, and partly about generational change, with the public spiritedness of the wartime generation in the USA giving way to a more private younger generation, which is less socially committed. In the last couple of years, I have been involved in a project that is trying to explore whether or not the same trends are to be found in Britain. British research is more ambivalent than its American counterpart because, as a political scientist called Peter Hall has argued, we do not find the trend towards disengagement working in quite the same way in Britain as we do in the USA, and some forms of political association linked to concern about the environment have actually increased in Britain. We find this in growing membership of organisations such as Greenpeace, the National Trust, and others with rural and environmental concerns. However, what we are finding very clearly in Britain is the withdrawal of the working class from civic life. Twenty years ago, there was not much difference between the likelihood of working class and middle class people joining clubs and associations; basically, the average working class person belonged to 1 association and the average middle class person belonged to 1.2 associations, so there was no real class gradient in terms of whether or not people were involved in voluntary associations. Now, middle class people are still likely to join voluntary associations, but working class people have mostly dropped out. We see increasing middle class predominance in all forms of public and social life: this is equally true of voluntary work for charities, involvement with political parties, or membership of church groups.

Most remarkable is what has happened to the trade union and labour movements. The trade unions and the

Labour Party developed historically mainly to look after the interests of manual workers, and the bulk of their membership consisted of people from the manual working class, working in heavy industries, factories, coal mines and so forth. Trade union membership has fallen off a great deal in the last twenty years and the groups that are most likely to be represented by a trade union are no longer industrial workers, but professional groups such as doctors, teachers and nurses. Overall, middle class professionals are now more likely to be in a trade union than those in manual work. Those manual workers who are in trade unions, such as fire fighters, are most likely to be in the public sector. The same point is also true of the Labour Party. In the past, the Labour Party always had a lot of middle class activists, but there were always also a significant number of working class activists, because of the role of the trade unions and through community groups. Today, about 80% of Labour Party activists are from the professional and managerial ranks and so the historic link between the Labour Party and the working class has largely collapsed.

These seem to me to be really quite serious changes, because what has been created is a vicious circle, in which there is a kind of overlap between middle class work and public life. People who are in professional or managerial jobs can use their work skills as they go in to public and civic life. Generally speaking, professionals know how to speak in a public setting, chair meetings, write minutes and organise formal activities and these skills can be applied to civic and similar associations. This, of course, makes it more difficult for people without these skills to feel that they belong in this sort of association. In the past, there was much more diversity in the way associations and organisations operated and there was much more debate about norms and how they should be organised. Now, it is assumed that there is only one way of organising this type of activity, which basically draws upon unstated middle class assumptions about how things should be done: that is, formally, in accordance with the aims and objectives of the association, with things being transparent, etc. Although it may seem obvious to people in middle class jobs that this is the best way to organise, there are many people without these skills who end up feeling that they do not actually know how to participate in these forms of public or civic life. Their response, therefore, is to opt out. We now live in a society in which working class membership has fallen across the board, but particularly in trade unions; even membership of working men's clubs has fallen considerably. The important issue here is that this sort of drop-out is often seen as not being of any significance. It is regarded as an individual matter. The fact that people drop out because they feel that they are inadequate and do not have the skills or the capacities to take part in these associations and organisations is not seen as a political issue, but as a matter of individual failing.

Conclusions

To conclude, let us consider the concept of social inclusion-exclusion. There is clear evidence that our society is fundamentally polarised and that this polarisation is continuing, even under a Labour government. Essentially, this is not about discrimination against a few particular types of people; it is much more fundamental and structural than that. In many ways, Marx's argument that there is a fundamental cleavage, a fundamental division between capital and labour, is borne out by these developments. This leads to the second point, which is that in this respect Tony Blair, John Major and Margaret Thatcher are absolutely correct in their perception that people on the whole do not think of themselves as members of classes. Their senses of identity are much more complex than that. The paradox of class is that there really is not a link between people's objective class distinction, their awareness of class, and what used to be called the base and the superstructure of society. What has happened in this situation is not that class has ceased to matter or that class culture is no longer important, but that certain middle class norms, which were at one time contested, have become the unstated assumptions around which social life is organised. It has come to be taken for granted that things should be done in a certain way, following protocols and values which middle class people are better able to participate in by virtue of their educational background. Therefore, we find working class people and those from ethnic minority backgrounds dropping out of social and political life. However, they do not think that their drop-out is to do with structural reasons, but see it as an individual problem, even though in fact it is to do with fundamental class divisions. In terms of the title of this conference - are we here seeing discrimination or inequality? In my view, we are in the final analysis seeing inequality in terms of class.

References

Charlesworth, S. J. (2000). *A phenomenology of working class experience.* Cambridge: Cambridge University Press.

Putnam, R. D. (2000). *Bowling along: The collapse and revival of American community.* New York: Simon & Schuster.

Savage, M. (2000). *Class Analysis and Social Transformation.* Buckingham: Open University.

Savage, M., Bagnall, G., & Longhurst, B. (2005). Globalization and belonging. London: Sage.

Skeggs, B. (1997). *Formations of class and gender: Becoming respectable.* London: Sage.

UK Department of Employment. (1991). *New earnings survey [1991].* London: HMSO.

UK Office of National Statistics. (1998). *New earnings survey [1998].* London: Author.

6

DISABILITY, DISCRIMINATION AND DISABLED PEOPLE

Colin Barnes

Introduction

For most of the twentieth century, disability in most "Western" societies has been associated with "flawed" bodies and minds. Generally perceived as an individual medical problem, the term was associated with a whole range of conditions and illnesses that may or may not affect people's capabilities and functioning. These include physical and sensory impairments, such as paralysis, "blindness" and "deafness", and cognitive conditions like "learning difficulties" or "mental illness". People labelled "disabled" were seen as somehow inadequate and not "normal", and viewed as dependent and a "burden" to their families, their friends, and the state. In short, disability was construed as a "personal tragedy" and a social problem for the rest of society.

This is somewhat surprising, given that people with accredited impairments have existed in all societies throughout history and that the more technically and socially sophisticated societies become, the more "disability'" they create. Recent estimates suggest that there are about 8.2 million disabled people in Britain, 50 million in the European Union, and 500 million worldwide. These figures are set to rise substantially in the coming decades, both in the rich "developed" countries of the minority world and in the poorer "underdeveloped" nations of the majority world (International Disability Foundation, 1998). This is due to a variety of factors, including medical advances, ageing populations, the intensifying pace of technological and social change, violence and war (Albrecht, Seelman, & Bury, 2001).

Recently, however, orthodox wisdom regarding disabled people has been challenged. Since its politicisation by disabled activists in the 1960s, disability has become an increasingly important political issue for politicians and policy makers at both the national and international levels (Campbell & Oliver, 1996). Many national governments now have some form of anti-discrimination law or policy to promote the rights of disabled people (Barton, 2001). It is unlikely, however, that these measures alone will eradicate the various barriers – economic, political and cultural – to inclusion encountered by disabled people. This is because discrimination against disabled people is institutionalised in the very fabric of Western society and is evident in all areas of economic and cultural activity (Barnes, 1991).

To illustrate this claim, this chapter is divided into three main sections. The first will define the type of discrimination encountered by disabled people. The second will document the extent of this discrimination in key areas, including history and culture, abortion and abuse, education, employment and the built environment. Attention will then turn to disability politics, discrimination and the limitations of the law.

Definitions and Terminology

To understand the complexity of the discrimination encountered by disabled people, it is helpful to begin with a discussion of the redefinition of disability by disabled people and their organisations. Historically, people with ascribed impairments have been defined in a variety of different, and often derogatory, ways by religious leaders, politicians, policy makers and professionals in order to mark them out from the rest of society in different contexts and in different cultures (Stiker, 1999).

In an effort to minimise confusion, during the 1970s the World Health Organization (WHO) commissioned a team of social scientists to develop the existing "International Classification of Disease" to cover the consequences of "long-term illness". The result, "The International Classification of Impairment, Disability and Handicap" (ICIDH), was published in 1980. Widely regarded as the most comprehensive catalogue of its kind, it has been used as a basis for Government initiatives on disability in both the rich countries of the minority world of Europe and North America, and the poorer, "developing" nations of the majority world of the South and East.

The ICIDH uses a threefold typology of "impairment", "disability" and "handicap". Thus, impairment refers to "any loss or abnormality of psychological, physiological or anatomical structure or function". Disability denotes "any restriction or lack (resulting from an impairment) of ability to perform an activity in the manner or within the range considered normal for a human being". Handicap is the "disadvantage for a given individual, resulting from an impairment or disability that limits or prevents the fulfilment of a role that is normal (depending on age, sex and social and cultural factors) for that individual" (WHO, 1980, p. 29).

Clearly, this construct is based on notions of intellectual and physical "normality", and the assumption that disability and handicap are caused by psychological or physiological "abnormality" or impairment. However, there is substantial evidence that perceptions of impairment and normality are social phenomena that are not easily defined, and are subject to substantive temporal, cultural and situational variation (Ingstad & Whyte, 1995). Dyslexia, for example, would not be viewed as a major problem in an agrarian society. Yet it is considered an important learning difficulty in modern, technically advanced societies such as Britain and the USA, where literacy and numeracy are necessary prerequisites for economic and social participation.

Indeed, the word "normal" entered the English language about 1840: coincidently, at the same time that the pressures of industrialisation were forcing governments to define, classify and control "deviant" populations (Davis, 1995). Moreover, implicit in the ICIDH is the assumption that the human body is flexible and adaptable, whilst the physical and/or social environments are not. This clearly flies in the face of reality, since historically humans have always moulded the environment to suit their needs rather than the other way round (Barnes, 1991). Additionally, the ICIDH definitions suggest that impairment, disability and handicap are static states. Apart from the fact that this is inaccurate, it creates distinctions and barriers between people, those with or without impairments, where there need not and should not be any (Sutherland, 1981). Such a situation is particularly ludicrous, given that the ICIDH has a classification for every feature of human physicality (Shakespeare, 1994a, 1994b).

Moreover, besides reflecting a particularly narrow set of Euro-centric values, the ICIDH has provided neither consistency nor clarity. For example, in addition to the above, the ICIDH defines handicap as "a discordance between the individual's performance or status and the expectations of the group of which he (sic) is a member"; the same could be said of both impairment and disability, making consistency of usage very difficult (Oliver & Barnes, 1998, p. 16).

Finally, impairments are presented as the primary cause of disability and handicap, which therefore should be "cured" by medical intervention. People with impairments are seen as objects to be treated, changed, improved and made "normal". While medical intervention to treat illness and disease may be quite appropriate, it is increasingly argued by a growing number of disabled people that it cannot address the problem of disability (Brisenden, 1986). The perception is due mainly to the fact that disabled people and their organisations were not involved in the development of the ICIDH schema.

The first definition generated by an organisation controlled exclusively by people who actually experience disability was produced in 1994, six years before the publication of the WHO typology. It was developed in Britain by the Union of the Physically Impaired Against Segregation (UPIAS) and adopted a two-tier construct. As with the ICIDH, the term impairment focuses on the biological: namely, "lacking all or part of a limb, or having a defective limb, organism or mechanism of the body". But: "Disability is something 'Imposed on top of our impairments by the way we are unnecessarily isolated and excluded from full participation in society'. Disabled people are therefore an oppressed group in society" (UPIAS, 1976, p. 14). This approach was later adopted and adapted by many organisations controlled and run by disabled people themselves, including, in 1981, Disabled People's International (DPI) – the international umbrella for national organisations controlled and run by disabled people, to encompass all forms of impairment, whether physical, sensory or cognitive (Driedger, 1989).

Moreover, this distinction has facilitated the construction of a "social model" of disability that centres on the various environmental barriers - economic, physical and cultural - that inhibit disabled people from

Disability, Discrimination and Disabled People

participating in mainstream society on a par with non-disabled peers (Oliver, 1983). From this perspective, therefore, "disability" represents a particularly complex and pervasive form of social oppression or institutional discrimination that operates at the general level of society or the state, and is supported by history and culture. Thus:

> It incorporates the extreme forms of prejudice and intolerance usually associated with individual or direct discrimination, as well as the more covert and unconscious attitudes which contribute to and maintain indirect and/or passive discriminatory practices within contemporary organizations. Examples of the influence of institutional discrimination upon social policy include the organization of the education system and the operation of the labour market, both of which are influenced by government and both of which perpetuate the disproportionate economic and social disadvantage experienced by disabled people. It is evident therefore that, within this frame of reference, direct, indirect and passive discrimination are not easily distinguishable concepts, but are intertwined in most contexts. (Barnes, 1991, p. 3).

Although there is not the space to deal with it here, for particular sections of the disabled population, such as disabled women, disabled members of minority ethnic groups, and disabled lesbians and gay men, the problem of institutional discrimination is compounded by institutionalised sexism, racism, heterosexism and homophobia.

Institutional Discrimination and Disabled People

While there is substantial anthropological evidence to suggest that cultural responses to perceived impairments are not universal, negative attitudes and practices towards people with designated impairments have pervaded Western culture since the ancient world of Greece and Rome (Stiker, 1999).

The Greeks and Romans idealised youth and fitness and were enthusiastic advocates of infanticide for sickly or weak infants. Indeed, in the Greco/Roman world, biological arguments were the justification for all forms of inequality (Garland, 1995). The dread of impairment was reinforced by examples from the Bible, which suggested that abnormalities of the body and mind were punishments for past sins. This negative picture was perpetuated by the denunciation of newly born children with impairments as "changelings", or inhuman beings, and evidence of parental involvement in witchcraft, by a succession of medieval clerics from St Augustine to Martin Luther. There is also ample data showing that these views permeated everyday life and popular culture, and that impairment was a source of ridicule, fear and pity. Furthermore, this cultural legacy remains with us today and finds expression in a variety of classical and popular media and forms, and provides the bedrock upon which discrimination and prejudice rest (Hevey, 1992).

Although discrimination was prevalent across medieval Europe, it was fragmented and took many forms. It became more institutionalised as a consequence of the economic and social upheavals that accompanied industrialisation. Indeed, the growing importance of economic rationality, liberal utilitarianism, and medical science during this period contributed to and compounded ancient fears and prejudices and provided the intellectual justification for relatively more extreme practices. This included the systematic removal of large numbers of people with any form of physical or cognitive abnormality from the mainstream of economic and social life.

People with impairments were ill-equipped to compete for wages in the factories of the industrial age. Those who were unable or unwilling to conform to the newly dominant ideologies of the period, namely self-reliance and the work ethic, were categorised and incarcerated into institutions such as asylums, hospitals and workhouses by a burgeoning bureaucracy and medical profession, eager to establish their worth in a rapidly changing and increasingly competitive world.

These policies were given added impetus with the publication of Darwin's theory of evolution in 1859 and its application to human development by academics such as Herbert Spencer and Francis Galton. With the spread of social Darwinism and eugenic ideas for "improving the human race" (Abrams, 1968, p. 49), any form of accredited impairment became a threat to human progress. The logical outcome of this was "social hygiene" policies for the mass segregation and medically sponsored sterilization and abortion of people with impairments across Europe and North America. In 1938, thirty-three American states had a law allowing the forced sterilisation of women with intellectual impairments, but in Nazi Germany during the 1930s and 1940s an altogether more systemic and extensive extermination programme was introduced against "unworthy life". This led to the murder of over 270,000 disabled people regarded as "travesties of human form and spirit" (Burleigh, 1994, p. 194).

Since the mid-twentieth century, however, there has been a general "softening" of attitudes and a definite attempt to "integrate" disabled people into community life in most Western societies. To facilitate this goal, there has been a rapid expansion of community-based support services and professional helpers. While the positive effects of these developments are not in doubt, it is clear that they rest on traditional perceptions of impairment and disability. Discrimination has not disappeared; it has simply been transformed into more subtle and less obvious forms.

Probably the most significant example of the continued influence of traditional assumptions about impairment and disability can be found in current debates about abortion, euthanasia, violence and abuse; all of which, to varying degrees, question the value of disabled people's lives.

In many countries, campaigns to legalise abortion explicitly reaffirm societal attitudes toward physical and cognitive abnormality. For example, Britain's 1967 Abortion Act states that pregnancy may be legally terminated at any time if it threatens the health of the pregnant woman or if there is a "substantial risk" that the child "would suffer from such physical and mental abnormalities as to be seriously handicapped". Women are often put under enormous pressure by doctors and families to abort a pregnancy once impairment is detected (Thomas, 1997). Such pressure is justified on the grounds that a disabled child is an emotional and financial "burden" on both the family and the state. Moreover, these views underpin the work of many "scientists"' involved in the development of genetic medicine. This is clearly reflected in the following statement by Professor Bob Edwards, made to delegates at the European Conference on Human Reproduction and Embryology in 1999: "Soon it will be a sin for parents to have a child that carries the heavy burden of genetic disease. We are entering a world where we have to consider the *quality* of our children" (quoted by Rogers, 1999). Despite the fact that the overwhelming majority of impairments are acquired rather than hereditary, there is little doubt that such assertions devalue the very existence of everyone with a recognised impairment and in so doing undermine their legitimate demands for equal rights and opportunities.

Furthermore, recent debates about the legalisation of euthanasia also pose a direct threat to disabled people's existence. While the medical profession has been formally opposed to "mercy killing", in cases where there is agreement that the quality of life is unacceptable, a person's life may be terminated with medical approval, perhaps after discussion with the patient or the family. Once legalised, as now in the Netherlands, there will be growing pressure on people with "severe" impairments to opt for euthanasia: (see "Lives not worth living?" [*Disability Tribune*, August 2000]).

Violence and abuse, emotional, sexual and physical, is significantly and routinely directed at disabled people both individually and as a group. It is a particular feature of the lives of disabled children and women in institutions (Stanley, Manthorpe, & Penhale, 1999). Sweden sterilised 60,000 women between 1935 and 1976, including many with learning difficulties. Similar eugenic-inspired laws were passed in Finland, Denmark, Switzerland and Japan. Yet such policies are frequently and widely overlooked, on the grounds that disabled people's lives are of lesser value than non-disabled contemporaries (Sobsey, 1994).

Discrimination is endemic to contemporary education and employment systems. Formal education is geared for two main activities. These are: first, the dissemination of dominant social values considered necessary for active citizenship; and second, the allocation and selection of people for participation in the labour market. Segregated "special" education systems for disabled children are present in most Western societies. Support for segregated provision comes from a variety of sources, including policy makers, professionals, parents and some sections of the disabled community. It is argued that mainstream schools are unable to provide the high levels of health and individualised educational support and empathetic peer culture needed by children with "special educational needs". Advocates maintain that segregated schooling is more efficient and effective, because scarce and costly resources, such as specialist teachers and equipment, can be concentrated in segregated school environments (Corbett, 1998).

Segregated schooling has long been the preferred option of deaf people and their organisations, as it is the only way to ensure both the continuity of deaf culture and non-aural communication systems, and that children with hearing impairments grow up with a positive self-identity and therefore able to participate effectively in a predominantly aural society. This has created a deep division between organisations of deaf people and most other organisations of disabled people, who believe that the special education system is deeply implicated in the oppression of people with impairments and should be abolished (Corker, 1998).

Critics maintain that removing disabled children from family, peers and the local community has wide-ranging negative implications (Morris 1997). Residential and segregated institutions inhibit disabled children's ability to make friends with non-disabled peers. In special schools, impairment considerations often take priority over educational ones. Lower expectations amongst educationalists and teachers often mean that disabled children are exposed to a limited curriculum.

Consequently, the academic achievement of pupils in these environments is well below that of their non-disabled peers.

In Britain, disabled children from "special" schools leave with fewer qualifications and marketable skills than their non-disabled peers, so that working age disabled people are "more than twice as likely on average than non-disabled people to have no formal qualifications" (Christie, 1999, p. 89). While Government documents proclaim their broad commitment to deliver "excellence for all children" (UK Department for Education and Employment [DfEE], 1998), the education system is geared increasingly to competition, choice and selection. Strategies include a national curriculum, and published league tables with performance indicators of educational attainment and examination results. In this policy environment, disabled pupils are perceived as a liability. Similar patterns of lower educational achievement among disabled children compared with their non-disabled peers exist around the world. In Canada and Australia, this is widely documented at both secondary and university levels (Chouinard, 1997; Gleeson, 1999).

In most modern societies, paid work is probably the most important criterion for categorising people in terms of class, status and power. Consequently, those on the margins of the labour market encounter a variety of economic, political and social deprivations.

Although unemployment rates vary over time and between countries, except in times of war, this is a common experience for disabled people of working age. In 1999, it was stated that "disabled people are seven times as likely as non-disabled people to be out of work and claiming [welfare] benefits" (Christie, 1999, p. 89). The unemployment rate for disabled Americans in the mid-1990s stood at 13.4 %, or more than twice the level for non-disabled peers (LaPlante, Kennedy, Kaye, & Wenger, 1996). The figures for Australia tell a similar story (Gleeson, 1999).

Disabled people are particularly under-represented in the professions and management, where there are higher earnings, job security and opportunities for promotion. Conversely, disabled people are over-represented in low skilled, poorly paid, less secure jobs (Roulstone 1998). In Britain, disabled men working full time earned on average 25% less than their non-disabled counterparts, while the wages of disabled women were only two-thirds that of disabled men (Burchardt, 2000). In both Australia and Canada, disabled employees earn about 30% less than their non-disabled equivalents (Gleeson, 1999). Similarly, in the USA, disabled workers earn only 64% of the average non-disabled income, in large part because of lower hourly wages and fewer hours worked (LaPlante et al., 1996). Within the disabled population, those identified as people with learning difficulties or with a "mental illness" experience much greater work disadvantages (Barnes & Mercer, 2003).

This can be attributed to several factors. In Britain, for example, there is consistent and persuasive evidence of negative practices and attitudes towards the employment of disabled workers among both employers and workmates. Inaccessible transport and workplaces and inflexible working conditions provide significant barriers. The increasing emphasis on formal qualifications, marketable skills, medical screening, and a "socially acceptable" appearance by employers further contribute to the discrimination against groups within the disabled population (Barnes, 1991; Burchardt, 2000). Similar patterns have been identified across Europe and North America (Thornton, Sainsbury, & Barnes, 1997; US

National Institute on Disability and Rehabilitation Research [NIDRR], 2000).

An important outcome of this situation is that the majority of disabled people in Western countries experience higher levels of poverty and are more reliant on state welfare payments or charity for financial support. In Britain, state welfare benefits are the sole source of income for three-quarters of all disabled adults. Indeed, around 45% of disabled Britons live below the official poverty line (Berthoud, Lakey, & McKay, 1993), while in the USA 30% of disabled people of working age are classified as living in poverty. The rate is even higher amongst specific sections of the disabled community, rising to 72% for disabled women with children under 6 years (LaPlante et al., 1996, p. 2). Moreover, individuals with an impairment have higher costs simply because society is geared to the needs of non-disabled people. This is reinforced by expenditure on impairment-related items, such as specialised equipment, personal clothing, heating, transport and housing adaptations (Berthoud et al., 1993).

It is also worth noting that social and economic inequalities are reflected in the consumption of services. In those countries with significant public and private welfare sectors, the reliance on public rather than private sector provision (in such areas as housing, transport and education) has been an important mark of social status. In practice, most disabled people remain disproportionately reliant on the state and voluntary sectors, while they are further differentiated as a result of their segregation in special schools and housing (Barnes & Mercer, 2003).

Institutional discrimination against disabled people is perhaps never more apparent than in the built environment – housing, transport and public space. Examples include:

- physical barriers to movement for disabled people, including broken surfaces on thoroughfares (streets, guttering, paving) that reduce or annul the effectiveness of mobility aids (e.g. wheelchairs, walking frames);
- building architecture which excludes the entry of anyone unable to use stairs and hand-operated doors;
- public and private transport modes which assume that drivers and passengers are non-impaired; and
- public information (e.g. signage) presented in forms that assume "a common level of visual and aural ability" (Gleeson, 1999, p. 137).

Until recently, urban infrastructures were designed with little or no thought for the needs of people with recognised impairments. An inaccessible built environment has a knock-on effect for a wide range of activities, including the choice about where and when to work, type and location of housing, and participation in leisure activities. This in turn inhibits earning and shopping opportunities, while also leading to higher travel costs and investment of more time in making the necessary alternative arrangements (Barnes & Mercer, 2003).

Although most Western societies now have some form of legislative framework with which to address inaccessible built environments, these policies have been slow to make an impression on discriminatory urban design. For example, Britain's 1970 Chronically Sick and Disabled Persons (CSDP) Act instructed local authorities to address the access needs of disabled people with regard to housing, public buildings, schools and universities. In the early 1970s, local authorities' "completions" of wheelchair adaptable dwellings rose substantially, but thereafter declined dramatically to a handful in the 1990s. Moreover, despite the rhetoric of "social inclusion" that pervades recent official publications, segregated "special needs" housing remains central to Government plans for "community care". In Britain, homelessness among the disabled population is relatively high and particularly so among mental health system users and "survivors" (Sayce, 2000).

Inaccessible public transport systems, including buses, trains, coaches and aeroplanes, also provide major barriers to social and economic participation for disabled people. This is particularly disempowering, as large sections of the disabled community, such as blind people, are unable to drive, and because many disabled people who are able to drive cannot afford the relatively high costs of motoring.

Disability Politics, Discrimination and the Law

The politicisation of disability and the struggle for equality initially became clustered around the notion of rights in the USA in the late 1960s. The Black civil rights struggles, with their combination of conventional lobbying tactics and mass political action, had an important influence on America's emergent "Disability Rights Movement" (Hahn, 1987). By contrast, Britain's early disabled people's movement, in the form of the Disablement Incomes Group (DIG), formed in 1965 by two disabled women, adopted a more conventional route. This is partly due to the fact that, unlike the USA, Britain had no written constitution or, until 1998, human rights legislation, but a well-established farrago of disability charities and voluntary organisations, run by professionals and non-disabled people, that favoured a more orthodox paternalistic approach. Also, in 1970 the British Government had introduced the comprehensive CSDP Act, mentioned above, which at the time promised far more than it delivered.

Decoding Discrimination

Until the mid-1970s, the American Disability Rights Movement was a loosely structured amalgam of grass roots groups and organisations. The combination of increasing demonstrations by overtly political groups, such as New York's "Disabled in Action", and lobbying within Congress by sympathetic legislators, resulted in the insertion of disability related provisions into the 1973 Rehabilitation Act.

In common with Britain's 1970 CSDP Act, this legislation included sections on environmental access, improved employment opportunities and more comprehensive services, including user-led initiatives known as Centres for Independent Living (CILs). It also included the historic Section 504. This is important because, for the first time, it prohibited discrimination against disabled people in any federally funded programme.

However, local, state and federal governments were reluctant to implement Section 504 and this generated further action amongst those aiming to affect policy change at federal and state levels and those concentrating on grass-roots initiatives. Additionally, there were increased legal battles involving disabled individuals seeking redress for the denial of their constitutional rights. This attracted considerable media attention and heightened public awareness of the struggles for disabled people's rights, eventually culminating in the Americans with Disabilities Act (ADA) of 1990 - the oldest and most comprehensive anti-discrimination legislation in the world (Doyle, 1999).

Rooted in a culture of "absolute individual rights", the ADA set out to "mainstream" disabled Americans as fully as "practicable". Its rationale is based on an antipathy to "paternalistic state institutions", dependence, and the notion that disabled people's "empowerment and self-sufficiency" can be achieved "through remunerative employment" (Bickenbach, 1999, p. 105). The ADA outlawed discrimination against disabled people in employment, transport and the built environment, state and local government, and telecommunications. It has encouraged notable improvements in the accessibility of the built environment, but, as we have seen, its effects in other areas have been much less than anticipated.

The independent US National Council on Disability (NCD), in its examination of the enforcement activities, found that:

> While the Administration has consistently asserted its strong support for the civil rights of people with disabilities, the federal agencies charged with the enforcement and policy development under ADA have, to varying degrees, been under-funded, overly cautious, reactive and lacking any coherent and unifying national strategy. In addition, enforcement agencies have not consistently taken leadership roles in clarifying "frontier" or emergent issues.
>
> (Bristo, 2000, p. 1).

Specific concerns have been expressed about the ADA's slowness, the weaknesses of its monitoring and enforcement provisions and its impact on minority groups within the disabled population. Moreover, the onus is on the disabled person to seek "reasonable accommodation". In practice, the overwhelming majority of cases are settled out of court, with 95% of the remainder decided in favour of the employer (NCD, 2000).

Nevertheless, its passage symbolised a significant shift in the perception of disabled people in the USA and became the exemplar for anti-discrimination legislation in other countries through the 1990s, including the Australian Disability Discrimination Act (1992), the inclusion of disability discrimination within a Human Rights Act in New Zealand in 1993 and Britain's 1995 Disability Discrimination Act (Doyle, 1999).

Since the 1970s, British organisations controlled and run by disabled people, such as the UPIAS, the Liberation Network and Sisters Against Disability (SAD), have pursued similar goals to their American peers. An important stimulus for these campaigns was the setting up of the Committee on Restrictions against Disabled People (CORAD) by the Labour Government in 1978, which was chaired by a disabled person, Peter Large. This committee's report, published in 1982, included a recommendation for legislative action to combat discrimination, but the newly elected Conservative Government of Margaret Thatcher ignored it. In July 1982, a deaf Labour MP, Jack Ashley, introduced a private member's anti-discrimination bill, but Parliament rejected the motion (Barnes & Mercer, 2003).

As a consequence, the campaign for anti-discrimination legislation gathered momentum during the 1980s. In 1985, the Voluntary Organisations for Anti-Discrimination Legislation (VOADL) Committee, renamed Rights Now in 1992, was established. This provided an uneasy alliance between organisations controlled and run by disabled people and the more traditional paternalistic organisations *for* disabled people, which had, hitherto, been unsympathetic to the arguments for an anti-discrimination law. This was also a period of growing politicisation and activism amongst disabled people. This led to the development of Disability Equality Training (DET), an approach to consciousness-raising based on the social model of disability, and direct action and demonstrations by disabled activists and their supporters across the country. Important milestones include the "Rights Not

Charity" March of July 1988, the demonstrations against the exploitation of disabled people on television by charity shows such as Telethon 1990 and 1992, and the formation of the Disability Direct Action Network in 1993 (Campbell & Oliver, 1996). By the mid-1990s, all Britain's major political parties acknowledged the need for legislation. The Conservative Government introduced a bill in 1994 that became the Disability Discrimination Act (DDA) of 1995.

As with the ADA, the DDA is based on an individual, medical approach to disability. For example:

> A person has a disability for the purposes of this Act if he or she has a physical or mental impairment which has a substantial or long-term adverse effect on his (sic) ability to carry out normal day to day activities. (DDA., 1995).

Moreover, the individual must demonstrate that they have an impairment before litigation can begin. Under the terms of the Act, discrimination occurs when disabled people experience "less favourable treatment" without good cause and when "reasonable" adjustments are not made. The law provides only limited protection from direct discrimination in employment, the provision of goods and services, and in the selling or letting of land. Moreover, although recently included, initially education and transport were not covered by the Act.

From the outset, employers' organisations were opposed to comprehensive disability rights legislation. They argued that, unlike comparable initiatives for women and minority ethnic groups, removing environmental and cultural barriers to disabled workers would have enormous financial implications for the business community. This may explain why over 90% of employers were initially exempted from the Act, as they employed fewer than 20 people (Gooding, 2000). This exemption has recently been amended to cover those with fewer than 15 employees.

Moreover, unlike the ADA, the DDA began life without an enforcement agency to monitor its implementation. This was also unlike other British anti-discrimination legislation, such as the 1975 Sex Discrimination Act (SDA), with the Equal Opportunities Commission (EOC), and the 1976 Race Relations Act (RRA), with the Commission for Racial Equality (CRE). The situation was only resolved in 2000, with the establishment of the Disability Rights Commission (DRC). Following the 1997 election and its pre-election promise to introduce new legislation, New Labour set up the "Disability Rights Task Force". It produced a report in 1999 that identified the need for a commission to police the DDA. This, combined with intense lobbying by disability organisations, led to the establishment of the DRC.

The DRC has the power to take up cases on behalf of both individuals and organisations. However, early indications suggest that, like the EOC and the CRE, its main activities will revolve around the production of new codes of practice, the updating of existing ones, the provision of information and advice, conciliation, and research (UK Disability Rights Commission, 2002). This is because, although formally "independent", government-appointed commissions such as the EOC and CRE are limited in what they can achieve, as funding and appointments are subject to ministerial control. As a result, the bulk of their activities revolve around "education and research" rather than regulation and enforcement, thus rendering them relatively ineffective (Bagilhole, 1997).

The question of equity for disabled people was also recognised in 1996, when the European Commission

Disability, Discrimination and Disabled People

adopted a directive on equal opportunities for disabled people. Its aim was to "encourage", rather than require, member states to abolish segregated facilities in favour of mainstreaming for disabled people. Additionally, a clause to counter discrimination against various groups, including disabled people, was written into the revised Treaty on European Union in 1997. The European Union in October 2000 agreed to a directive requiring member states to introduce anti-discrimination legislation in a number of areas, including disability, while 2003 has been declared the European Year of Disabled Citizens.

The passage of the Human Rights Act 1998, as well as the impact of European Community law, is likely to have a further influence on UK disability politics. This may yet lead to disabled people and their organisations following a similar path to that favoured by their counterparts in other Western countries, with intensified campaigns for increased civil rights through the law courts. However, the legislative route is limited in what it can achieve. It is lengthy, expensive, favours particular sections of the disabled population and detracts attention away from the economic, political and cultural environment in which the legal system operates; and, therefore, away from the very forces which created and now sustain discrimination against disabled people and, indeed, anyone unable or unwilling to conform to Western values and norms. Furthermore, there is a growing consensus amongst disability scholars and activists that meaningful inclusion for people with accredited impairments, and other economically and socially disadvantaged groups, is only possible through deep-rooted and radical changes to the way our society is organised (Barnes, Oliver, & Barton, 2002).

Conclusion

This chapter has demonstrated that, in contemporary "Western" society, the level of social participation experienced by disabled people in key areas of everyday life is severely constrained by various barriers: economic, political and cultural. The data shows that, to varying degrees, this phenomenon is the outcome of Western economic and cultural development; in particular, the intensifying material and cultural changes generally associated with the eighteenth and nineteenth centuries. Whilst the policy extremes of the first half of the twentieth century have largely given way to more subtle and socially acceptable forms, this legacy remains with us today; discrimination against people labelled "disabled" is endemic in everyday life. It is also evident that, although legislation has been introduced to address this problem, its impact has been limited. Furthermore, this unfortunate situation is unlikely to change without deep-rooted structural and cultural change, involving the systematic redistribution and allocation of resources and the generation of a culture that celebrates rather than rejects human diversity.

Indeed, impairment is not something that is peculiar to a small section of the population; it is an inevitable part of the human experience. Discrimination against people perceived as "disabled" is, like sexism, racism and all the other forms of social oppression that characterise present-day society, a social creation. It is impossible, therefore, to confront one type of oppression without confronting them all and, of course, the various forces which created and now sustain them.

As we move further into the twenty-first century, the reality of this insight becomes ever more obvious.

References

Abrams, P. (1968). *The origins of British sociology, 1834-1914: An essay with selected papers.* Chicago: University of Chicago Press.

Albrecht, G. L., Seelman, K. D., & Bury, M. (Eds). (2001). *The disability studies handbook.* Thousand Oaks, CA: Sage.

Australia Statutes (1992). *Disability Discrimination Act, No. 135, 1992.* Barton, ACT: Office of Legislative Drafting and Publishing.

Bagilhole, B. (1997). *Equal opportunities and social policy: Issues of gender, race, and disability.* London: Longman.

Barnes, C. (1991). *Disabled people in Britain and discrimination: A case for anti-discrimination legislation.* London: Hurst & Co., in association with the British Council of Organizations of Disabled People.

Barnes, C., & Mercer, G. (2003). *Disability.* Cambridge: Polity Press.

Barnes, C., Oliver, M., & Barton, L. (Eds.). (2002). *Disability studies today.* Cambridge: Polity Press.

Barton, L. (Ed.). (2001). *Disability, politics & the struggle for change.* London: David Fulton.

Berthoud, R., Lakey, J., & McKay, S. (1993). *The economic problems of disabled people.* London: Policy Studies Institute.

Bickenbach, J. E. (1999). Minority rights or universal participation: The politics of disablement. In M. Jones & L. A. B. Marks (Eds), *Disability, divers-ability and legal change* (p. 101-115). The Hague: M. Nijhoff.

Brisenden, S. (1986). Independent living and the medical model of disability. *Disability, Handicap & Society, 1,* pp. 173-178.

Bristo, M. (2000). Letter of transmittal. In US National Council on Disability, *Promises to keep: A decade of federal enforcement of the Americans with Disabilities Act.* Washington DC: US National Council on Disability.

Burchardt, T. (2000). *Enduring economic exclusion: Disabled people, income and work.* York: YPS, for the Joseph Rowntree Foundation.

Burleigh, M. (1994). *Death and deliverance: "Euthanasia" in Germany, c. 1900-1945.* Cambridge: Cambridge University Press.

Campbell, J., & Oliver, M. (1996). *Disability politics: Understanding our past, changing our future.* London: Routledge.

Chouinard, V. (1997). Making space for disabling differences: Challenging ableist geographies. *Environment and Planning D: Society and Space*, 15 (379-387.

Christie, I., with Mensah-Coker, G. (1999). *An inclusive future? : Disability, social change and opportunities for greater inclusion by 2010.* London: Demos.

Corbett, J. (1998). *Special educational needs in the twentieth century: A cultural analysis.* London: Cassell.

Corker, M. (1998). *Deaf and disabled, or deafness disabled: Towards a human rights perspective.* Buckingham: Open University Press.

Darwin, C. (1859). *On the origin of species by means of natural selection, or, The preservation of favoured races in the struggle for life.* London: John Murray.

Davis, L. J. (1995). *Enforcing normalcy: Disability, deafness, and the body.* London: Verso.

Doyle, B. (1999). From welfare to rights? : Disability and legal change in the United Kingdom in the late 1990s. In M. Jones & L. A. B. Marks (Eds.), *Disability, diversability and legal change* (pp. 209-226). The Hague: M. Nijhoff.

Driedger, D. (1989). *The last civil rights movement: Disabled People's International.* London: Hurst.

EU Treaties (1997). *Treaty of Amsterdam amending the Treaty on European Union, the treaties establishing the European Communities and certain related acts.* Luxembourg: Office for Official Publications of the European Union.

Garland, R. (1995). *The eye of the beholder: Deformity and disability in the Graeco-Roman world.* London: Duckworth.

Gleeson, B. (1999). *Geographies of disability.* London: Routledge.

Gooding, C. (2000). Disability Discrimination Act: From statute to practice. *Critical Social Policy, 20,* 533-549.

Hahn, H. (1987). Civil rights for disabled Americans: The foundation of a political agenda. In A. Gartner and T. Joe (Eds.), *Images of the disabled, disabling images* (pp. 181-203). New York: Praeger.

Hevey, D. (1992). *The creatures that time forgot: Photography and disability imagery.* London: Routledge.

Ingstad, B., & Whyte, S. R. (Eds.). (1995). *Disability and culture.* Berkeley: University of California Press.

International Disability Foundation. (1998). *World disability report.* Geneva: Author.

LaPlante, M. P., Kennedy, J., Kaye, H. S., & Wenger, B. L. (1996, January). *Disability and employment* (Abstract 11). Retrieved June 29, 2005, from the University of California San Francisco, Disability Statistics Center On-line: http://dsc.uesf.edu./pub_listing.php?pub_type=abstract

Lives not worth living? (2000, August). *Disability Tribune*, 1-2.

Morris, J. (1997). Gone missing? : Disabled children living away from their families. *Disability & Society, 12*, 241-258.

NZ Statutes. (1993). *Human Rights Act, No. 82, 1993.* Wellington: Government Printer.

Oliver, M. (1983). *Social work with disabled people.* London: Macmillan.

Oliver, M., & Barnes, C. (1998). *Social policy and disabled people: From exclusion to inclusion.* London: Longman.

Rogers, L. (1999, July 4). "Having disabled babies will be a sin", says scientist. *The Sunday Times*, p. 1/28b.

Roulstone, A. (1998). *Enabling technology: Disabled people, work and new technology.* Buckingham: Open University Press.

Sayce, L. (2000). *From psychiatric patient to citizen: Overcoming discrimination and exclusion.* Basingstoke: Macmillan.

Shakespeare, T. (1994a). Cultural representation of disabled people: Dustbins for disavowal? *Disability & Society, 9,* 283-299.

Shakespeare, T. (1994b). [Review of the book *Disabling barriers – Enabling environments*]. *Disability & Society, 9,* 103-104.

Sobsey, R. (1994). *Violence and abuse in the lives of people with disabilities: The end of silent acceptance?* Baltimore: P. H. Brookes Publishing.

Stanley, N., Manthorpe, J., & Penhale, B. (Eds.). (1999). *Institutional abuse: Perspectives across the life course.* London: Routledge.

Stiker, H-J. (1999). *A history of disability* (W. Sayers, Trans.). Ann Arbor: University of Michigan Press. (Original work published 1982).

Sutherland, A. T. (1981). *Disabled we stand.* London: Souvenir Press.

Thomas, C. (1997). The baby and the bathwater: Disabled women and motherhood in social context. *Sociology of Health and Illness, 19,* 622-643.

Thornton, P., Sainsbury, R., & Barnes, H. (1997). *Helping disabled people to work: A cross-national study of social security and employment provisions: A report for the Social Security Advisory Committee.* London: Stationery Office.

UK Committee on Restrictions Against Disabled People. (1982). *Report.* London: Department of Health and Social Security.

UK Department for Education and Employment. (1998). *Excellence for all children: Meeting special educational needs.* London: HMSO.

UK Disability Rights Commission. (2002). *Disability Discrimination Act 1995: Code of practice; rights of access; goods, facilities, services and premises.* London: Stationery Office.

UK Disability Rights Task Force on Civil Rights for Disabled People. (1999). *From exclusion to inclusion: A report.* London: Department for Education and Employment.

UK Statutes. (1967). *Abortion Act: Elizabeth II, 1967, Chapter 87.* London: HMSO.

UK Statutes. (1970). *Chronically Sick and Disabled Persons Act: Elizabeth II, 1970, Chapter 44.* London: HMSO.

UK Statutes. (1975). *Sex Discrimination Act: Elizabeth II, 1975, Chapter 65.* London: HMSO.

UK Statutes. (1976). *Race Relations Act: Elizabeth II, 1976, Chapter 74.* London: HMSO.

UK Statutes. (1995). *Disability Discrimination Act: Elizabeth II, 1995, Chapter 50.* London: HMSO.

UK Statutes. (1998). *Human Rights Act: Elizabeth II, 1998, Chapter 42.* London: Stationery Office.

Union of the Physically Impaired Against Segregation, and Disability Alliance. (1976). *Fundamental principles of disability: Being a summary of the discussion held on 22nd November, 1975 and containing commentaries from each organization.* London: Author.

US National Council on Disability. (2000). *Promises to keep: A decade of federal enforcement of the Americans with Disabilities Act.* Washington DC: Author. Also available at: http://www.ncd.gov (retrieved June 29, 2005).

US National Institute on Disability and Rehabilitation Research. (2000). *Long range plan.* Washington, DC: Author.

US Statutes. (1973). *Rehabilitation Act of 1973, Public Law 93-112.* Washington, DC: Office of the Federal Register.

US Statutes. (1990). *Americans with Disabilities Act of 1990, Public Law 101-336.* Washington, DC: Office of the Federal Register.

World Health Organization. (1980). *International classification of impairments, disabilities and handicaps: A manual of classification relating to the consequences of disease.* Geneva: Author.

7

REBELLIOUS SUBCULTURES: FASHIONING THE REVOLUTION IN A REVOLTIONARY FASHION OR VEHICLES OF RESISTANCE EN ROUTE TO CONFORMITY?

JOANNA ELLOY

The concept of rebellious subcultures is intriguing. On the surface, they are perceived as rebellious forces, defying mainstream culture through the diversification of their sense of style, their music and their development of alternative sets of beliefs and even lifestyles, whilst managing to maintain their existence within mass culture.

The very term "*sub*culture" implies something below the standard of mass culture; an undesirable element of society. Indeed, mass culture seems to fear certain subcultures, often as a result of media-inspired moral panics (Cohen, 1987). This has sometimes resulted in discrimination against and even criminalisation of specific activities of particular subcultures: for example, the legislation that was introduced to make the congregation of groups of New Age Travellers illegal, and the outlawing of raves in the 1990s (McKay, 1996).

It is possible however, that capitalism, one of the aspects of hegemonic society that rebellious subcultures are believed to be resisting through their very existence, is the power that fuels the spread of subcultural style. Conversely, it is possible that capitalism has absorbed styles of resistance, transmogrifying them into mainstream phenomena as a means of social control. It is these possibilities that this paper will focus upon, investigating whether or not subcultural style is paradoxically coerced into conformity via the capitalist process, or conversely, if deviant subcultures have in fact used capitalist ideology to assert their dissatisfaction with the system. These possibilities are made more complex by perspectives that assert that we exist in the postmodern era, the ideology of which exerts plurality, flux and heterogeneity (Muggleton, 2000).

The first section of the paper will briefly attempt to define the term "mass culture" and then examine the concept of the rebellious subculture, endeavouring to contextualise it in terms of its relationship with mass culture. During this process, the concept of deviance will also be touched upon, to highlight the negative vein in which rebellious subcultures are perceived. This established, the paper will investigate the significance of style, attempting to ascertain the extent to which subcultural styles are routes of resistance or merely diverse manifestations of the postmodern era, created by the evolution of mainstream culture. Finally, the paper will examine the relationship between rebellious subcultures and capitalism and discuss the postulation that capitalism is either the manipulator or the manipulated within the relationship. Ultimately, it will aim to provide a clearer understanding of the issue of whether or not the rebellious styles of deviant subcultures are merely alternative routes to conformity, manipulated and endorsed by a discriminatory capitalist system.

What is a Rebellious Subculture?

Foucault's concept of discourse can be seen to provide a framework for considering how society's rule-making occurs, and how "truths" are constructed via various semiotic processes, such as language, images and practices. These "truths" then become habitualised, sedimented and institutionalised (Berger & Luckmann, 1967) and consequently become naturalised, which makes them difficult to challenge (Giles & Middleton, 1999). Nevertheless, challenges do occur, and those who instigate such challenges are often perceived as rebellious subculturalists. It has been argued, however, that in order to understand deviant behaviours, it is first necessary to understand the conforming path from which they diverge (Deutscher, 1962). The aim of this section is therefore to outline briefly the meaning of "culture", and then to examine the concept of "subculture", contextualising it in terms of its relationship with and its place within mass culture.

Williams (1976), cited in Giles and Middleton (1999, p. 9), describes the term culture as "one of the two or three most complicated words in the English language", and goes on to provide three possible definitions:
- A general process of intellectual, spiritual and aesthetic development.
- A particular way of life, whether of a people, a period, a group, or humanity in general.
- The works and practices of intellectual and especially artistic activity.

Williams appears to suggest that the term culture implies a shaping process: i.e. that members of any given society learn to adopt certain beliefs and to behave in a particular way. Indeed, Bauman, cited in Abbott (1998), uses the analogy of a garden to describe culture, as both are cultivated. To develop this analogy, it could be suggested that rebellious subcultures have been perceived as the weeds in the garden, which need to be pulled out and disposed of. The definitions offered by Williams, however, appear to be somewhat ambiguous, and it would be quite straightforward to apply them to the concept of mass culture or of subculture. Indeed, learning or socialisation theory asserts that deviant behaviour is learned in the same way as normal behaviour: i.e. through the process of socialisation (Giddens, 1997). In applying this perspective to rebellious subcultures, it could be suggested that those individuals who interact with existing subculturalists will learn their beliefs and behaviours and thus become integrated into the subcultural way of life. Similarly, those who learn such beliefs and behaviours via the mass media may adopt the behaviours that are broadcast as negative qualities, thus defeating the object of media-created moral panics. For example, Garratt (1997) writes that the media-created punk image of "foul mouthed, violent, moronic yobbos" influenced emergent punks to behave in a similar vein, as they had learned that this was how punks were supposed to behave. From this, it could be concluded that certain subcultures are, in fact, creations of media-inspired moral panics and are, as Garratt implies, far removed from their original ideals. However, this learning theory has been criticised. Clinard & Meier (1998) imply that learning theory negates individual autonomy, categorising those who adopt a subcultural lifestyle as a generalised mass, incapable of personal and rational decision-making. Taylor (1971) criticises the theory as being too simplistic, arguing that people are not at the mercy of information fed by external sources, but are autonomous beings, able to process information received and to take an active, rather than a passive, role in determining what to do with that information. Brake (1985) suggests that culture may be a source of general guidance for most people with regard to compliant behaviour and beliefs, but that subcultures, by their very existence demonstrate that there are alternative lifestyles, thus "reflecting cultural plurality in a culture" (Brake, 1985, p. 8). Brake appears to imply that culture per se, or "mass culture", is the "norm", i.e. the conformist way of life, but that it is the individual's choice either to conform with or deviate from the norm.

It has been said that subcultures are perceived negatively as "deviant": "Their shadowy, subterranean activities contrast dramatically with the 'enlightened' civil decencies of the 'public' " (Thornton, 1997a). This is an interesting point, which raises important issues regarding the unacceptability of such alternative lifestyles. Cohen (1971) writes that deviance from the norm is indeed socially perceived as a negative concept, and uses words such as "brutal", "vicious" and "degenerate" to illustrate his point. However, he goes on to say that the concept of deviance is much more generic: for example, being diverse or to digress. Deviance, then, could be said to be "anything that differs from what is most common" (Becker, 1973, cited in Garratt, 1997). The very word "subculture" when dissected has negative connotations. The prefix "sub", according to the definition of the *Collins English dictionary* (1989) implies something that is beneath, secondary to, or below standard; thus, to look at the word in its entirety is to be immediately informed that a subculture is beneath, secondary to, or below the standard of mass culture. Sociologists, however, despite often suggesting that subcultures are the product of subordinated working class people in protest, are careful to apply no such secondary status to a subculture when offering a definition. For example, Clarke, Hall, Jefferson & Roberts (1975) state that, for a subculture to be recognised as such, it must differ significantly from its parent culture. Thornton (1997a) suggests that a subculture consists of a group of people who share common values, which differ substantially from those of mainstream society. Such definitions however, although recognising the integrally diverse elements of subcultures, neither explain how they came into existence nor why they have been perceived in such a negative way.

A suggestion put forward by Merton is that subcultures are the product of an arguably distorted reflection of society's aspirations for status. Status is synonymous with success, which has often eluded the lower classes, and the implication is that it is the lower classes that are most likely to make deviant adaptations (Clinard & Meier, 1998). Merton's development of Durkheim's theory of anomie can be applied here: i.e. the encouragement of society's members to attain certain standards, such as material assets. The inequality of social conditions, however, makes it impossible for all members actually to achieve these goals, perhaps because of unequal educational and employment opportunities (Taylor, 1971; Aggleton, 1987; Little, 1995; Clinard & Meier, 1998). The symbolism of success is often displayed in an individual's style; thus, the rebellious subculturalists' decision to use such symbolism as a vehicle of protest seems poignant in a capitalist culture in which great emphasis is placed upon material gain. Frow (1995, p. 11) makes this point when defining the concept of subculture as "a term that designates the tightly knit identity of a social group bonded above all by a ... highly loaded choice of stylistic markers". The post-war years saw for the first time an affluent working class youth, with the means to achieve the power of status that money can buy (Abrams, 1959 cited in Frith, 1984; Davis, 1990; Garratt, 1997). This new affluent youth led to the construction of the concept of the "teenager", which Frith (1984) and Garratt (1997) suggest may possibly have evoked fear and envy from adults, for whom such freedom in the transition from childhood to adulthood was unknown. This fear, exacerbated greatly by media-inspired moral panics, contributed to exhibitions of difference during the establishment of youth identity being frowned upon and demonised. Indeed, the moral panics resulting from the Mods and Rockers incidents during the 1960s are testament to the realisation by mass culture that the allegedly unacceptable behaviour exhibited by subculturalists, as reported by the media, were not executed by lower class people, but by affluent members of society: "These were not just the slum louts whom one could disown, but faintly recognisable creatures who had crawled out from under some very familiar rocks" (Cohen, 1987, pp. 194-195). Frith (1984) suggests that some of this fear may also be attributed to working class people's fear that the new teenage culture not only reflected affluence, but also the decomposition of the pre-war working class community. This appears to have become something of a pattern in the development of various subcultures: they have at first been regarded as articles of interest and then, as the result of media-inspired or at least exacerbated public fear, have been metamorphosed into folk devils. For example, Davis (1990) states that the appearance of the hippie subculture was regarded with amusement by both the general public and the media, the latter of which featured headlines such as: "March of the Flower 'Pot' Men" *(Daily Mirror*, July 17, 1967, cited in Davis, 1990, p. 200). Brake (1985) demonstrates the shift in public perception of the hippie subculture, stating that they rapidly became folk devils, described by the media as "wilfully idle, promiscuous, dirty and drug using vagrant[s]" (Brake, 1985). Latey (1967), cited in Davis (1990), points out that the demonisation of the Mods and Rockers subcultures by the media may have been inaccurate, stating that the five hundred youths who vandalised a seaside town made headline news, whereas the scores of thousands who led ordinary lives were ignored.

Rebellious Subcultures

Rebellious subcultures have also been construed as a means of attempting to incite revolution and anarchy. This accusation remains bound up in the Marxist class conflict theory of working class subordination by hegemonic society, and can be demonstrated by the punk subculture, which, it has been argued, declared anarchic war on the establishment; for example, the non-coincidental timing of the release in the year of Elizabeth II's Silver Jubilee of the Sex Pistols' single, "God Save The Queen", the lyrics of which, according to John Lydon, "…meant something; they weren't just done for shock value: they had a purpose" (Callanan, 2002). However, this assertion has been opposed by sociologists who argue that diverse dress, music and lifestyles are not enough to cause a revolution. Marsh (1982, p. 163) argues that the idea that the songs of punk rock were designed to cause anarchy is absurd: "The lyrics are unintelligible …. If this is the way in which revolution is to be preached, we are all going to need printed song sheets". Some sociologists have also argued that subcultures, in their semiotic resistance to mainstream society, have in fact merely offered "magical" or "imaginary" solutions to the ideology of mass culture (Brake, 1985; Clarke et al., 1975). This assertion appears to imply that members of rebellious subcultures do not have the power to make any dramatic changes in society, but can only use semiotic resistance to make their dissatisfaction with mass culture apparent. Of course, it could be counter-argued that it cannot be assumed that all subculturalists wish to incite dramatic change and that instead they are content to live alternative lifestyles whilst remaining cocooned in mainstream society. Clarke et al. (1975) appear to support this argument, stating that, although subculturalists project diverse cultural responses or solutions to the problems posed by their position in society, they share the same fundamental and determining life experiences as their "parent" culture.

Many of the assertions regarding the development of rebellious subcultures appear to rest upon class conflict theories. These theories perceive society as a collection of groups with competing interests in conflict with one another (Clinard & Meier, 1998) and assume that members of rebellious subcultures are of working class origin. However, it must be noted that this is not necessarily an irrefutable fact. The hippie subculture, for example, has been said to have middle class origins (Frith, 1984; Brake, 1985). Distler (1970), cited in Brake (1985, p. 93), argues that the hippie subculture represented "a flight from a patristic, instrumental culture to a matristic, expressive one", and goes on to say that its drug use was symbolic of a disregard for normal society and its values. Frith (1984) states that middle class subcultures were more self-consciously rebellious than those of working class origin, as they opposed their very roots, whereas working class people merely drifted into deviance as a result of confusion, because of lack of discipline. This is an extremely narrow-minded point of view, however. Brake appears to be negating the experiences of working class people, implying via a gross generalisation that they are valueless and immoral. Aggleton (1987) supports this argument, stating that the actions of punks, bikers and skinheads were far from being "mindless" and "illogical". Instead, Aggleton argues that these were actually rational responses to being young in a class-divided society, in which birth status affects life chances, providing certain opportunities for the upper classes, whilst denying them to the lower classes. However, he goes on to say that the rebellious actions taken by these subcultures ultimately served to reinforce class divisions rather than challenge them: see, for example, Clarke's (1995) study of the culture of skinheads, whose actions and style were an attempt to "'magically re-create' the threatened working class community" (Aggleton, 1987, p. 85). It is also a matter of contention as to whether the punk subculture was in reality a class-based phenomenon. Aggleton cites Peter Marsh (1982, p. 165) as dubbing punk "dole-queue rock", as its lyrics reflected working class frustrations. However, he counter-argues that punk "attracted young people from across the social spectrum" (Aggleton, 1987, p. 86). Hebdige (1979) argues that it may be an oversimplification to attribute the deviant actions of punk to class-based issues per se, and suggests that far more complex social issues need to be considered.

The discussion thus far has demonstrated that rebellious subcultures are complicated phenomena and many definitions of them seem to rest on Marxist class conflict theory, although this is arguable. What does appear to be a recurrent theme, however, is that mass culture is a route to conformity, while subcultures represent diversity and deviance from the norm. This has not been perceived favourably by mainstream society, which seems to fear that the symbolism displayed by rebellious subcultures acts as a thinly veiled threat to civilised society. This raises the issue of the methods employed by the relatively powerless against Becker's "moral entrepreneurs" of society, and it seems that the use of style has been a powerful tool in registering dissatisfaction and disillusionment with the system. It is this stylistic form of protest that will be the focus of the next section.

The Significance of Style in Rebellious Subcultures

It can be seen that rebellious subcultures are perceived as being deviant from society's norms and that they are therefore non-conformist. As such, they have largely been regarded negatively by mainstream society. Furthermore, the general method of resistance employed by rebellious subcultures is largely of a semiotic nature; in particular, it consists of the styles which various subcultures adopt and which become specific, and indeed indicative of their particular subculture (Brake, 1985). Hebdige (1979, p. 18) sums this up succinctly, asserting that: "Style in subculture is ... pregnant with significance". Here, the paper will examine the said significance of this sartorial rebellion, whilst endeavouring to discover the extent to which style is employed as an effective form of resistance and also to examine the methods used to make style signify rebellion at all.

Bricolage

Levi-Strauss's concept of "bricolage" means the re-contextualisation of existing objects to create new meanings (Clarke, 1975). This acts as a stylistic challenge to the hegemony of the dominant culture (Barker, 2000; Muggleton, 2000), which has been strongly suggested to be the main cause of the incitement of rebellious subcultures, as discussed in the preceding section. The concept of bricolage enables ordinary everyday items to become objects of shock and fascination. Frith (1984) supports and develops this suggestion, stating that the subcultural re-appropriation of objects serves not only to shock, but also to threaten the usual stability of imagery: "Punk ... turned style inside out" (Walker, 1982, p. 9). Hebdige (1979, p. 104) uses the examples of the motor scooter, originally a "respectable" everyday means of transport, turned by the mod bricoleurs into a "menacing symbol of group solidarity", and of their metal combs, made razor sharp, which he somewhat playfully describes as narcissism as an offensive weapon. The employment of bricolage seems to be apparent in almost every rebellious subculture: the punks' re-appropriation of safety pins, bin liners, and even glue to symbolise a violent challenge to the social norms of middle class mass culture (Ives, 1987; Abbott, 1998) provides an illustration of this, as does the adoption of "upper class" Edwardian suits by the working class Teddy Boys to symbolise social revolt (Fyvel, 1963). The skinheads' cropped hairstyles and heavy boots, dubbed "bovver boots", underlined their violent reputation, which was associated with a style that represented an exaggerated working class image, reflecting fears of the loss of traditional working class culture in the face of economic decline (Clarke et al., 1975; Abbott, 1998). There is a strong implication of working class rebellion manifested through the use of bricolage in these descriptions. However, Frith (1984) argues that, to make this assumption, one must assert that style relates specifically to working class experience and also that style is purely a political response to these experiences. Neither of these assertions can be unequivocally proven. For example, the hippie subculture is said to have been a middle class phenomenon (Frith, 1984; Brake, 1985). Additionally, it has been argued that style is a medium of expression which, although it may be political in essence, can also represent a key element in people's self-exploration (Jones, 1990).

Homology

The concept of homology sees a given subculture as a set of "constitutive relationships ... [to] ... the objects, artefacts, institutions and systematic practices of others which surround it" (Willis, 1978, cited in Barker, 2000, p. 324). This suggests that it is not just style per se, but the amalgamation of a number of factors that give a more holistic picture of what makes a subculture. Clarke et al. (1975) develop this idea by incorporating it into the concept of bricolage, discovering that re-appropriated objects reflect subjective aspects of a group's life. For example, to look at the punk subculture holistically, it could be suggested that the dyed Mohican hairstyles, ripped clothes, safety pins, pogo dance, foul language and practice of glue-sniffing homologically contribute to the punk ideology of frustration, despair and anarchy. However, Hebdige (1979) raises the issue of the symbol of the swastika, worn by many punks, and questions its significance. He suggests that the swastika was another symbol subjected to the act of bricolage, as the punk subculture was not a fascist entity. Conversely, Hebdige also theorises that the swastika represented the punks' interest in "a decadent and evil Germany – a Germany which had no future " (p. 116) and he goes on to suggest that, for the British, the swastika conventionally signified the enemy. This would go some way to explain why the punk subculture selected it as being of semiotic value. Of course, the swastika has been interpreted within such subcultural analysis in terms of the fascist symbol associated with Hitler's atrocities, but it must be recognised that this is an act of bricolage in itself, as the meaning associated with the swastika for thousands of years prior to Hitler's despotic regime was that of the quest for enlightenment (Cainer & Rider, 1986). Therefore, it could be argued that the punk subculture was using the symbol in its original and entirely positive sense and that the negative connotations associated with it were the result of a prejudiced and ignorant mass culture. However, this argument is as speculative as the argument that it is meant to criticise and as such it may be sufficient to say that the key to the punk style remains elusive (Hebdige, 1979).

Postmodernism

It has been argued that the postmodern meaning of style represents heterogeneity, plurality and flux, as opposed to the modernist meaning of stasis, homogeneity and demarcation (Muggleton, 2000). Rebellious subcultural style therefore could be said to be a postmodern entity, striving to differ from homogenous mass culture, with the various subcultures asserting themselves as diverse, innovative groups (Hebdige, 1979). The contemporary interpretation of postmodern style, however, does not seem to allow for deviation from the norm to be perceived as rebellious. It is said to involve bricolage, but without reference to the objects' original meanings, consisting solely of the "look" without the underlying message or ironic transformation (Barker, 2000). "Retro-chic" imagery has been apparent in recent years, with the rapid re-surfacing of fashions from bygone eras such as the 1960s, 1970s and 1980s being dubbed the "recycling of authenticity" (Redhead, 1997); and while high street fashion retains a large following, it is no longer perceived as rebellious to deviate from this. Heterogeneity now appears to be the norm. Ironically, it could even be suggested that to conform one must display some form of diversity. For example, Thornton (1997b) states that, in the post-industrial world, consumers are encouraged to individualise themselves, although it should be recognised that such "individualism" remains in the hands of the mainstream clothes retailers from whom most individuals purchase their clothes. This suggests that style is no longer an avenue for rebellion, as any style may become socially acceptable and consequently have the potential to become the norm. This in turn raises the issue of social control, and it must be asked if the shift in the levels of acceptability of diverse styles is indicative of less social control over people's beliefs and lifestyles or of greater control exercised in a more subtle way. McRobbie (1989), cited in Barker (2000), argues against the suggestion of an apparent shallowness in contemporary society's adoption of bygone styles, stating that postmodern bricolage does not signify the end of meaning, but rather the forging of new meanings using existing objects. However, McRobbie does not appear to dismiss the notion that the contemporary diversity of style is manufactured by powerful "others", as she suggests that postmodern bricolage takes place via consumer capitalism, where the divisions between "authentic" and "manufactured" collapse. Muggleton (2000) suggests that this could transpire via the processes of diffusion and defusion. It must be remembered, however, that the "teenager" was a manufactured phenomenon. The creation of the affluent youth consumer in the post-war years was the result of young people having surplus money at their disposal (Clarke, 1975; Hebdige, 1979; Frith, 1984; Garratt, 1997). Thornton (1997b) supports the suggestion of manufactured youth, stating that youth culture is formed within and through the media, which is integral to the formation of subcultures. For example, Barker (2000) argues that there is nothing more likely to dull the pleasure of subcultural membership than media approval. Thus, if a record is banned and refused airtime, it can immediately become a sought-after commodity. This leads to the suggestion that rebellious subcultures are merely products of capitalist media manipulation, which adds another dimension to the question of whether or not rebellious subcultural styles are, somewhat ironically, actually endorsed by capitalism.

It has been demonstrated that subcultural style has been used as a method of resistance against mainstream culture and that it was also possibly utilised by the latter as a means of discrimination, leading to social control. Alternatively, it could be suggested that the significance of style has been exaggerated and taken out of context. Garratt (1997) suggests that rebellious style offers no real threat to society, as it is merely a symbolic gesture of dissatisfaction with the social order. Cohen (1980), cited in Barker (2000), argues that style has been over-inflated as resistance and manipulated to become only a political matter, while resistance has been reduced to merely a question of style. Thornton (1997b) also argues that youthful leisure has been over-politicised. However, it could be counter-argued that style has been only one of a number of semiotic modes of resistance employed by rebellious subcultures. Additionally, it must be argued that, if no significance is associated with particular styles, it is debatable as to whether anyone would dress in a specific way for any particular occasion; for example, black clothes worn at a funeral hold considerable significance and semiotic value. Clarke (1975) supports this argument, stating that styles re-appropriated by the bricoleurs to express their own lifestyles are only effective because they have been taken out of context from the meanings originally appropriated to them by the dominant culture.

It has also been claimed that rebellious subcultural style is in fact the product of capitalist media manipulation. This begs the question of how such styles are introduced and for what purpose? To what extent does capitalism play a role? Does the re-introduction of rebellious styles, but with their rebellious connotations removed, as with postmodern bricolage, signify a form of social control? These issues will be tackled in the next section, where the relationship between rebellious subcultures and capitalism will be examined in closer detail.

Decoding Discrimination

Rebellious Subcultures and Capitalism: a Manipulative Relationship?

The aim of this final section is to examine the role of capitalism with regard to the concept of rebellious subcultures. The discussion at this juncture will endeavour to discover whether or not rebellious subcultures are products of capitalism; if capitalism is manipulated by rebellious subcultures; or if, in fact, capitalism acts as a form of social control by promoting heterogeneity in the postmodern era, thus reducing rebellious subcultural style to alternative routes to conformity, endorsed by capitalism.

It has been suggested that consumption is one of the most basic ways in which contemporary society is formed (Hearn & Roseneil, 1999). This is in contrast to theories that stress the role of production in society. In developing this idea, some sociologists have also implied that the consumption of identity itself is indicative of the postmodern era, as identity and lifestyle have become commodified (Bocock, 1993; Munro, 1996; Chapman, 1999; Hearn & Roseneil, 1999). This suggestion almost implies that identity and lifestyle can be selected from high street stores; it would be an apt analogy in a society constructed around consumption. Giles & Middleton (1999) write of the ideology of consumption: i.e. the suggestion that we are denied identity in the process of production and as a result are forced to seek it via consumption. Great emphasis is therefore placed on the latter. We have become an "I consume therefore I am, rather than I consume because of what I am" society (Latimer, 2001, p. 161). Baudrillard (1981) argues that consumption is the purchase of signs, as opposed to commodities. Such a concept may be applied in contextualising the rebellious subcultural style in contemporary society, as it is now acceptable to adopt an enormous variety of styles which can be bought in the high street. As previously stated, diversity is paradoxically now the norm. Featherstone (1991) suggests that subcultures did operate symbolically, but that their semiotic resistance has now been either rejected or ironically parodied and collaged. However, the notion of the consumption of identity has been contested. Warde (1996) argues that it cannot be said that consumption plays an integral role in the formation of identity, and suggests instead that social location and involvement in social networks that enhance a sense of belonging play major contributory roles in the process of identity formation. It must also be argued that it is debatable as to whether style in the postmodern era incorporates identity, or whether it is an "empty vessel", consisting solely of the "look", without the underlying message (Barker, 2000). Featherstone (1991) opposes this argument, asserting that contemporary society is far from being symbolically impoverished, and goes on to say that consumer culture produces a vast array of signs, symbols and images. Featherstone cites Leiss (1978) to illustrate his point, stating that the symbolic associations of commodities serve to emphasise differences in lifestyle, which demarcate social relationships. While this may be a valid point regarding commodities in general, it remains highly questionable as to whether or not rebellious subcultural styles carry specific meaning in postmodern society. Ewen (1990) argues that style remains a critical factor of the self and asserts that it is a device of power, conformity and opposition. However, Ewen also counter-argues that rebellious style, dubbed "renegade style", has rebellious validity only for as long as it opposes the dominant imagery of mainstream society. Once it becomes absorbed into the capitalist market, as has been seen with some rebellious subcultures, it becomes demoted to mere style, as it no longer has rebellious connotations. Barker

(2000) asserts that the concept of contemporary subculture is questionable, as it is no longer situated outside mass-mediated consumer capitalism. Barker goes on to say that subcultures are now best understood in terms of "taste" rather than resistance. Using Ewen's argument, it could additionally be said that subcultural style also loses its power once its rebellious status has been lost. This argument is reflected in the development of punk rock music, which began with punks exhibiting a "do-it-yourself" ethic: "Punk prided itself on making recordings with all the rough edges showing" (Laing, 1990, p. 191). Punk used the production of music as one of many means of resistance against capitalist hegemonic society. Frith (1997) supports this suggestion, stating that punks challenged the capitalist control of mass music through their seizure of the technical means of music production. Conversely, however, it could be argued that the success of punk rock, leading to bands such as the Sex Pistols topping the charts, negated their resistance through music, as they became a mainstream phenomenon, in a way that is reminiscent of Weber's theory of the institutionalisation of charisma. Marsh (1982, p. 166) supports this argument, stating that a successful punk rock band "will have moved outside of the milieu which gives reason to its very existence. You can't play dole-queue rock and eat well at the same time". Similarly, Redhead (1997) writes that punk rock was swiftly incorporated and packaged for the youth culture market.

It could be argued that rebellious subcultures are actually a capitalist creation. It has already been strongly suggested that the "teenager" is a product of capitalism (Clarke, 1975; Frith, 1984; Davis, 1990; Garratt, 1997; Hebdige, 1997). Perhaps, then, the new affluent young people were targeted as means of profit-making, as they were the first generation to have surplus cash. The teenage phenomenon could be said to have developed via financial independence, leading to the purchase of the teenage identity, which symbolised independence from the parent culture. Indeed, Downes, cited in Davis (1990), states that the market has played a considerable role in sustaining youth in a position of high visibility throughout the post-war period. Capitalism could then be argued to have calculatedly provided both the incentive and the means of action for this to occur. Willis (1990) supports this suggestion, stating that capitalism is not only something from which to seek to escape, but also the means of that escape. This is done via the provision of an increasing supply of symbolic resources that can be appropriated to signify seemingly harmless resistance. Conversely, it has been argued that rebellious subcultures arose in response to capitalist hegemonic society (Clarke et al., 1975; Aggleton, 1987; Barker, 2000). It could therefore be argued that they were *incorporated into*, as opposed to *created by*, capitalism as a means of social control, making them a safe rather than a dangerous element of society. Hebdige (1979) claims that such incorporation of rebellious subcultures into mainstream society takes place via the commodification and redefinition of subcultures; for example, the manufacture of punk clothes by fashion companies, which sold them for a profit, such as McClaren & Westwood's shop "Sex" (Willis, 1990), and the redefinition of punks as "spirited" and "harmless" (Abbott, 1998). This then leads to the evolution of rebellious subcultures that have little or no meaning and, as Barker (2000) asserts, people adopt the "look" without the meaning. For example, Leech (1973, p. 4) writes of the commercialisation of the Mod scene, after which "phoney Mods began to be made". We live in a so-called "democratic society", which has to be seen to allow the freedom of speech and expression. The capitalisation of rebellious subcultures therefore enables this dubious theory to be perceived as actuality, while the danger of anarchy is defused. Indeed, the commodification of resistance has been said to be a hegemonic strategy (Garrison, 2000). It could therefore be suggested that capitalism has created an illusion of democracy. We imagine that we have the power to rebel semiotically, but in reality we remain in the trap of consumerism, as the objects that we use to symbolise our discontent with the system are simultaneously and ironically supporting it. However, this implies that we are "passive consumers", a view which questions the autonomy of the individual. Chambers (1986), cited in Frow (1995, p. 67), argues that rebellious subculturalists may instead have manipulated capitalism, using it to further their own ends. Chambers uses the example of the Mod subculture, in which, he argues, "consumerism was turned into the secret language of style, into imposing [their] presence on the goods". However, Frow (1995) suggests that such acts of bricolage beg the question of whether the subculture moulded the commodities, or if it rather functioned as a vehicle for commodity circulation. Redhead (1997) also suggests that capitalism has been the subject of manipulation, using the example of the singer Billy Bragg, who wrote songs exposing the negativity of capitalism whilst using capitalism to promote his work. However, it is a moot point as to which is the manipulator and which the manipulated, as money was undoubtedly made by and from Bragg.

    The discussion in this section has briefly highlighted the complexity of the relationship between rebellious subcultures and capitalism, exacerbated by their contextualisation in the postmodern era. It is clearly debatable as to whether style can be regarded as a method of semiotic resistance in contemporary society; so, indeed, is the question of whether it can be said to hold any significance at all. It has also been demonstrated that the aetiology of subcultures is greatly shrouded in uncertainty, raising questions about genuine resistance and manufactured resistance, which for the time being must remain unanswered.

Conclusion

This paper has shown that the making of rules in society essentially involves semiotic processes. It has been demonstrated that resistance to society's rules also quite aptly takes on a symbolic form, for example bricolage, often involving style. Rebellious subcultures are consequently negatively labelled by mainstream society as "deviant" and even dangerous, representing a thinly veiled and possibly anarchic threat to the social order. Style has therefore been argued to be a powerful tool in making subcultural resistance apparent.

The significance of style has been complicated, however, by the contextualisation of rebellious subcultures in the postmodern era, which exerts heterogeneity, plurality and flux (Muggleton, 2000). It has been argued therefore, that postmodern style involves bricolage, but without reference to the objects' original meanings. This can be seen in the recent and indeed rapid succession of "retro-chic" styles, emulating those of the 1960s, 1970s and 1980s. Here, postmodern style can be seen as the re-invention of the past, which adheres to the pessimism of postmodern ideology, asserting that there is no progress, and has even been said to fear the future, which "hints at a 'beyond' which it cannot name" (Beck, 1992, p. 9). This is in sharp contrast to the optimism of the modernist perspective. Perhaps then, disheartened postmodern society is attempting to recapture the air of excited anticipation of modernist times by reintroducing styles which have already been seen to hold considerable semiotic value. It has been argued however, that postmodern bricolage takes place via consumer capitalism (McRobbie, 1989, cited in Barker, 2000). This strongly suggests that today's wide variety of styles, all of which are potentially acceptable in heterogeneous postmodern society, are a subtle form of social control, as the vast array of mainstream fashions, somewhat ironically incorporating the rebellious styles of yesteryear, ensure that there is no avenue for resistance through style. Furthermore, there is no standpoint from which either side can effectively discriminate against the other. In simple terms, they have been "dumbed down" and rendered powerless. This paradoxical diversification of mainstream postmodern society, it has been suggested, provides the means for people to purchase their identities. If this is to be followed to its logical conclusion, it could somewhat flippantly be suggested that people may have several identities hanging in their wardrobes: "Everyone can be anyone" (Ewen & Ewen, 1982; cited in Featherstone, 1991, p. 83). It has been argued, however, that postmodern style lacks meaning; thus, the absorption of rebellious subcultures into mainstream culture by capitalism strips them of their power, thereby reducing them to matters of taste, as opposed to resistance. As has been argued, subcultural style only has rebellious status for as long as it opposes mass culture, for, upon absorption by mass culture, it becomes devoid of meaning (Ewen, 1990).

Another possibility that has been discussed is that rebellious subcultures are in fact a capitalist creation. It was suggested that capitalism calculatedly presents itself both as something from which to escape and also as the means for that escape (Willis, 1990). From this, it could be deduced that rebellious subcultures were created as profit-making pilot schemes for capitalism, which, if proved successful, would be released into the mainstream market. Apparent discrimination made manifest by media-inspired moral panics surrounding rebellious subcultures have generally been shown to *enhance* the spread of so-called rebellion. For example, many banned records immediately became sought-after commodities, thus providing support for this suggestion, demonstrating a tangled web of social control.

The concept of rebellious subcultural style has been seen to be extremely complex. Whether or not it is in fact an alternative route to conformity, endorsed by capitalism, cannot be determined from this study, as the precise roles that capitalism and rebellious subcultures play in the postmodern era cannot be definitively concluded. The complexity of the relationship between rebellious subcultures and capitalism is immense, and is greatly exacerbated by their contextualisation in postmodern society. To further the research carried out in this study, it would be necessary fully to investigate and provide an explanation of the concept of postmodernism, of which, ironically and perhaps by its own definition, there is as yet no agreed meaning. From there, issues of individualism, power and politics could be addressed, and this would enable the concept of discrimination to be explored from a more steadfast perspective and would allow us to determine whether or not it is, in fact, a tool, given to the masses by the powerful to use against one another as a means of social control, whilst defusing, diffusing and deflecting their attention away from what is really going on in the political world.

References

Abbott, D. (1998). *Culture and identity*. London: Hodder & Stoughton.

Aggleton, P. (1987). *Deviance*. London: Tavistock Publications.

Barker, C. (2000). *Cultural studies: Theory and practice*. London: Sage Publications.

Baudrillard, J. (1981). *For a critique of the political economy of the sign* (C. Levin, Trans.). St. Louis, MO: Telos Press. (Original work published 1972).

Beck, U. (1992). *Risk society: Towards a new modernity* (M. Ritter, Trans.). London: Sage Publications. (Original work published 1986).

Berger, P., & Luckmann, T. (1967). *The social construction of reality: A treatise in the sociology of knowledge*. London: Allen Lane.

Bocock, R. (1993). *Consumption*. London: Routledge.

Brake, M. (1985). *Comparative youth culture: The sociology of youth culture and youth subcultures in America, Britain and Canada*. London: Routledge.

Cainer, J., & Rider, C. (1986). *The psychic explorer*. London: Piatkus.

Callanan, M. (Producer). (2002, February 16). *Top ten banned singles* [Television broadcast]. Channel 4 Television.

Chapman, T. (1999). The ideal home exhibition: An analysis of constraints and conventions in consumer choice in British homes. In J. Hearn, & S. Roseneil, (Eds.), *Consuming cultures: Power and resistance* (pp. 69-90). Basingstoke: Macmillan Press.

Clarke, J. (1975). Style. In S. Hall, & T. Jefferson (Eds.), *Resistance through rituals: Youth subcultures in post-war Britain* (pp. 175-191). London: Hutchinson.

Clarke, J., Hall, S., Jefferson, T., & Roberts, B. (1975). Subcultures, cultures and class. In S. Hall, & T. Jefferson (Eds.), *Resistance through rituals: Youth subcultures in post-war Britain* (pp. 9-74). London: Hutchinson.

Clinard, M. B., & Meier, R. F. (1998). *Sociology of deviant behaviour.* (10th ed.). Forth Worth, TX: Harcourt Brace College Publishers.

Cohen, S. (Ed.). (1971). *Images of deviance.* Harmondsworth: Penguin.

Cohen, S. (1987). *Folk devils and moral panics: The creation of Mods and Rockers.* (New ed.). Oxford: Basil Blackwell.

Collins English dictionary. (2nd ed.) (1989). London: Collins.

Davis, J. (1990). *Youth and the condition of Britain: Images of adolescent conflict.* London: Athlone Press.

Deutscher, I. (1962). Some relevant directions for research in juvenile delinquency. In A. M. Rose, (Ed.), *Human behaviour and social processes: An interactionist approach* (pp. 468-481). London: Routledge & Kegan Paul.

Ewen, S. (1990). Marketing dreams: The political elements of style. In A. Tomlinson (Ed.), *Consumption, identity and style: Marketing, meanings, and the packaging of pleasure* (pp. 41-56). London: Routledge.

Featherstone, M. (1991). *Consumer culture and postmodernism.* London: Sage Publications.

Frith, S. (1984). *The sociology of youth.* Ormskirk: Causeway Press.

Frith, S. (1997). Formalism, realism and leisure: The case of punk. In K. Gelder, & S. Thornton (Eds.), *The subcultures reader* (pp. 163-174). London: Routledge. (Originally published 1980).

Frow, J. (1995). *Cultural studies and cultural value.* Oxford: Clarendon Press.

Fyvel, T. R. (1963). Fashion and revolt. In K. Gelder, and S. Thornton (Eds.), *The subcultures reader* (pp. 388-392). London: Routledge. (Originally published 1963).

Garratt, D. (1997). Youth cultures and subcultures. In J. Roche, & S. Tucker (Eds.), *Youth in society: Contemporary theory, policy and practice* (pp. 143-150). London: Sage Publications.

Garrison, E. K. (2000). U.S. feminism-grrrl style!: Youth (sub)cultures and the technologics of the Third Wave. *Feminist Studies, 26* (1), 141-170.

Giddens, A. (1997). *Sociology.* (3rd ed.). Cambridge: Polity Press.

Giles, J., & Middleton, T. (1999). *Studying culture: A practical introduction.* Oxford: Blackwell.

Hearn, J., & Roseneil, S. (Eds.). (1999). *Consuming cultures: Power and resistance.* Basingstoke: Macmillan Press.

Hebdige, D. (1979). *Subculture: The meaning of style.* London: Methuen.

Hebdige, D. (1997). Posing ... threats, striking ... poses. In K. Gelder, & S. Thornton (Eds.), *The subcultural reader.* (pp.393-405). London: Routledge. (Originally published 1983).

Ives, R. (1987). *The rise and fall of the solvents panic.* Milton Keynes: Open University.

Jones, S. (1990). Style, fashion and symbolic creativity. In P. E. Willis, *Common culture: Symbolic work at play in the everyday cultures of the young* (pp. 84-97). Milton Keynes: Open University Press.

Laing, D. (1990). Making popular music: The consumer as producer. In A. Tomlinson (Ed.), *Consumption, identity and style: Marketing, meanings, and the packaging of pleasure* (pp. 186-194). London: Routledge.

Latimer, J. (2001). All-consuming passions. In N. Lee, & R. Munro (Eds.), *The consumption of mass* (pp. 158-173). Oxford: Blackwell.

Leech, K. (1973). *Youthquake: The growth of a counter-culture through two decades.* London: Sheldon Press.

Little, C. B. (1995). *Deviance and control: Theory, research, and social policy.* (3rd ed.). Itasca, IL: F. E. Peacock.

McKay, G. (1996). *Senseless acts of beauty: Cultures of resistance since the sixties.* London: Verso.

Marsh, P. (1982). Dole-queue rock. In P. Barker (Ed.), *The other Britain* (pp. 159-166). London: Routledge & Kegan Paul.

Muggleton, D. (2000). *Inside subculture: The postmodern meaning of style*. Oxford: Berg.

Munro, R. (1996). The consumption view of self: Extension, exchange and identity. In S. Edgell, K. Hetherington, & A. Warde (Eds.), *Consumption matters: The production and experience of consumption* (pp. 248-273). Oxford: Blackwell Publishers.

Redhead, S. (1997). *Subculture to clubcultures: An introduction to popular cultural studies*. Oxford: Blackwell.

Taylor, L. (1971). *Deviance and society*. London: Joseph.

Thornton, S. (1997a). General introduction. In K. Gelder, & S. Thornton (Eds.), *The subcultures reader* (pp. 1-7). London: Routledge.

Thornton, S. (1997b). The social logic of subcultural capital. In K. Gelder, & S. Thornton (Eds.), *The subcultures reader* (pp. 200-209). London: Routledge. (Originally published 1995).

Walker, I. (1982). Skinheads: The cult of trouble. In P. Barker (Ed.), *The other Britain* (pp. 7-17). London: Routledge & Kegan Paul.

Warde, A. (1996). Afterword; the future of the sociology of consumption. In S. Edgell, K. Hetherington, & A.

Warde (Eds.), *Consumption matters: The production and experience of consumption* (pp. 302-312). Oxford: Blackwell.

Willis, P. E. (1990). *Common culture: Symbolic work at play in the everyday culture of the young.* Milton Keynes: Open University Press.